||| || ||||||| ||| ||||||| |||||

D0436744

ALSO BY TIM GUNN

Gunn's Golden Rules

Tim Gunn's Fashion Bible

TIM GUNN:
The Natty Professor

A Master Class on Mentoring,
Motivating, and Making It Work!

TIM GUNN
with Ada Calhoun

GALLERY BOOKS
New York London Toronto Sydney New Delhi

Gallery Books
A Division of Simon & Schuster, Inc.
1230 Avenue of the Americas
New York, NY 10020

First Gallery Books hardcover edition March 2015

GALLERY BOOKS and colophon are registered trademarks
of Simon & Schuster, Inc.

For information about special discounts for bulk purchases,
please contact Simon & Schuster Special Sales at 1-866-506-1949
or business@simonandschuster.com.

The Simon & Schuster Speakers Bureau can bring authors
to your live event. For more information or to book an event
contact the Simon & Schuster Speakers Bureau at 1-866-248-3049
or visit our website at www.simonspeakers.com.

Interior design by Jaime Putorti

Manufactured in the United States of America

1   3   5   7   9   10   8   6   4   2

Library of Congress Cataloging-in-Publication data is available.

ISBN 978-1-4767-8006-1
ISBN 978-1-4767-8008-5 (ebook)

5604 2061
3/15

To two remarkable teachers,
William Christenberry and Rona Slade,
who made more of an impact on who I became
than they can ever imagine

CONTENTS

CONTENTS

II. EMPATHY

III. ASKING

CONTENTS

IV. CHEERLEADING

V. HOPING FOR THE BEST

TAKEAWAYS

INTRODUCTION

MY T.E.A.C.H. PHILOSOPHY

My goal for this book is to start a national conversation about teaching. We talk all the time about the administration of education—test scores and Common Core, classroom size and teachers' unions—but what we don't talk about nearly enough is the single most important aspect of teaching, the key to determining whether knowledge is actually transmitted: the relationship between teacher and student. There's content and then there's methodology. The content will change, but good teaching is eternal.

I have been a teacher for more than half my life. Before my ten years as a mentor on *Project Runway*, I was for almost thirty years a classroom educator, and ultimately chair of the Parsons fashion design program. Despite the fact that I'm no longer in a classroom, I still consider myself first and foremost a teacher, and I try every day to become a better one.

When I started teaching, I bought three or four how-to books. I hated all of them. Some books on public speaking were useful, but I threw away all my teaching books and decided to just do what felt right. I made plenty of mistakes, but I also learned a lot.

In this book, as on TV, I want to share my experiences in the hopes that others may benefit. To me, this is a book of appreciation for those doing the important work of teaching. It's an *I-feel-your-pain* book, a cheerleading book, and a book that raises questions about what works best.

My view is that good teaching is all about asking questions driven by curiosity. It's about connecting with your students, not only as students but as fellow human beings. In order to give helpful and responsible instruction, you need context—as much information as you can elicit. If you don't know your students, how can you be sure that what you say will be meaningful for them?

I will add that asking questions of my class removed the sense of obligation I felt early in my teaching career to have all the answers on the first day. I realized over time that it was a journey we were on together. It wasn't up to me to do all the work. I came to realize that a class is a collaboration, as is life!

This past year I was lucky enough to host a *Project Runway* spinoff on Lifetime. *Under the Gunn* dealt with just this question of how to be a good mentor. On the show, I supervised three former designers—Mondo Guerra, Anya Ayoung-Chee, and Nick Verreos—as they learned to mentor younger designers.

On *Under the Gunn*, as the designers learned how to create innovative work under pressure, the mentors learned how best to guide the designers: to support them without coddling, to root for them without being blind to their faults, and to give them advice without being overbearing (or working on their garments—I'm looking at you, Nick!). The show was a fashion competition, but it also explored the question: What makes for a good teacher?

I am very sympathetic to struggling teachers. When I started out as a young design teacher, I had such bad stage fright that I threw up in the parking lot before class. Once in the classroom, I needed at times to grip the eraser ledge to keep from keeling over. Luckily, over time, the panic attacks stopped. I started to gain confidence. And I came to think of teaching as a calling. To see my students grow and mature and learn became for me the most important thing in the world.

When I became a department chair overseeing other teachers, I started to see more clearly how many different modes of teaching there were and to appreciate my colleagues' different styles. I also became convinced that certain methodologies were damaging, and bad teachers filled me with rage.

I think we all have stories about teachers whose influence on us was less than positive. One friend of mine had a second-grade music teacher who made her sing solos in front of the class to "cure" her shyness. No surprise, it did not work, but it did rob her of the enjoyment of music for years to come.

My miserable school years instilled in me a deep loathing for cruel teachers. I'm thinking of Mr. Allison—half a century later, I still remember his name—telling me to throw an eraser across the room. He thought I was too uptight. He charged himself with the task of making me break a rule. "Throw it!" he said, putting the eraser in my hand. I refused. It was humiliating. I'm sure he thought he was being very inspirational, but the reality was that he was only highlighting my anguish. And I had trouble recovering at that school. (I didn't last long there, or at any school. I bounced around like a kangaroo—a kangaroo in need of talk therapy and antidepressants.)

What the Mr. Allisons of the world commit is, essentially, teaching-malpractice. Shouldn't there be an educational equivalent of the Hippocratic oath? Breaching the oath would hold you accountable for your behavior, as it would with an M.D. Teachers who save us from ignorance should be given the glory (and income!) of open-heart surgeons. And yet, being such an unhappy student made me that much more grateful for those teachers who treated me with kindness and respect, or who showed me that I had value.

One day in elementary school, our art teacher handed out bars of soap and told us to carve anything we wanted. She probably just wanted to relax for an hour, but I took the assignment extremely seriously. Most of my classmates made ducks or other animals; I whittled the Governor's Palace from Colonial Williamsburg.

In addition to being, as it turned out, an excellent way to attract the attention of bullies, my soap palace taught me that I cared about architecture and construction in a way no one else in my class did. As hapless as I was at so many aspects of school (I had a terrible stutter, cried all the time, and often pretended to be sick so I could stay home), I knew, looking at that flaky little building, that there might be something I could do well after all.

I found every stage of my arts education liberating and life changing. At home, there were strict rules. My mother was so particular that she would object to my putting the knife and fork on the same side of the plate. When it came to art, there were no set rules, and the answer wasn't in the back of the book. What a revolutionary concept!

When I was at the Corcoran School of Art in 1974, the sculptor Anne Truitt taught me how to look at color and form in completely new ways. "Color has to sing from the inside," she said. "In order to do that, it has to have some transparency, and in order to give it that transparency, you can't use too much white, because that will kill it." She would talk about colors "zooming into being" when they were mixed.

Her passion for color was contagious. I'd never before thought about the power of a color to die or to zoom! Thanks to her, colors suddenly were characters to me. Anne taught me so much about life, too. She was a genuinely good person, and I found myself wanting more than anything to be like her. You saw this seriousness and integrity in her work, and in her life. The relationship between teachers and those they're teaching has almost boundless potential for transformation.

My decision to seek out Anne Truitt and study under her—not toward any kind of career goal, but because I simply loved her work and admired her as a person—put me where I am today. After graduation, I became a sculptor and builder of architectural models. Even though I eventually wound up in the field of fashion, the roots of my appreciation for fashion are in architecture. Some people believe in being "practical," and only studying things that will prepare us for the exact job we will have. But I believe that education should broaden our horizons. Nothing we learn that we care about is ever wasted.

So many people who do great things in life follow many different paths before ending up in the role that defines them, and none of that time is squandered if they're learning. The recently appointed director of the Smithsonian's Cooper Hewitt,

National Design Museum, Caroline Baumann, for example, got her master's degree in medieval art. While there are no knights or pietàs in her day-to-day work, that field trained her eye and her mind in a way that serves every aspect of her work. Another colleague of mine majored in the ancient Indian language Sanskrit and now writes for newspapers. Even though Sanskrit is no longer widely spoken, it helped my friend understand grammar. Not to mention, knowing that language offers her direct access to some of the most beautiful poetry in history.

One friend of mine had a writing teacher, Mrs. Price, who in sixth grade wrote in the margin of her *Great Expectations* book review that she was talented and should never stop writing. She did eventually become a writer, and now nearly thirty years later is still in touch with that teacher.

Another friend of mine tells me that the best class he ever took was a college class in Chaucer. Even though he went into a completely different field, he can still joyously recite parts of *The Canterbury Tales* (although he tells me there is not nearly the clamor for this at parties that you might expect), because his teacher made his students into lifelong Chaucer fans. Loving Chaucer doesn't necessarily make him a more valuable job candidate or help him win promotions, but it does make him a happier, more actualized human being. I expect he will take lines like, "And gladly wolde he lerne, and gladly teche," with him into his golden years.

Fashion designers certainly benefit from whatever else they've studied, whether it's a musical instrument, or a sport, or math. Any new information can help you craft your vision as a designer. Bradon McDonald of *Project Runway* Season 12, for example, knew intuitively how clothes would move on the body because of his years as a dancer. All designers would benefit from a physical practice. (Although please don't make me join you. I've never been in a gym, and the only sport I ever liked was swimming, because it's clean, quiet, and you don't sweat.)

Teaching is undervalued and underpaid in this country. To all the classroom teachers out there: bless you. To all the eager students and supportive schools and parents who make those teachers' lives easier and more fulfilling: bless you, too. In the course of a life spent trying to become a better teacher, I've come to believe that good teaching can be determined by five qualities. I love acronyms, so I'm giddy that these qualities fall neatly into what I've taken to calling my T.E.A.C.H. philosophy.

T stands for Truth Telling. A key role of the teacher is to inject reality into situations. As a fashion mentor, when a designer thinks he is making an elegant ball gown but is in fact making something that would be better in a three-ring circus, it is my job to say what I see. It is the teacher's job to tell us the cold, hard truth, because the world certainly will! Better to face our demons when we're in school and able to work on self-improvement full-time.

E stands for Empathy. As teachers, we need to have compassion for our students, to look at where they're coming from, and to intuit their particular strengths and limits. Not everyone has the same toolkit, and so not everyone is going to make the same kind of work. It's only by paying close attention to whom the students are and putting yourself in their shoes that you can truly help them. Teachers who try to make every one of their students into mini-me's are not doing anyone a favor.

MY T.E.A.C.H. PHILOSOPHY

A stands for Asking. The single-best teaching trick I ever learned was to turn every question back on the student. If a student asks, "Is this hemline too short?" I will say, "Do you think it's too short?" Nine times out of ten, the student will see exactly what you see, but when he comes to the realization himself, it is so much more valuable than when you force-feed it. I also find myself asking questions all day long, everywhere I go. The more curious you are about things, the more you get out of the world.

C stands for Cheerleading. In the *Project Runway* workroom, I tell designers to "Make it work," and to "Go! Go! Go!" And I point out areas in which they are strong. I celebrate their victories. Nothing feels better than the runway shows at the finale of *Project Runway* when I'm standing next to a designer watching a live feed of the show on a video monitor and the designer is weeping with pride. I am often crying right there with them!

H stands for Hoping for the Best. One of the hardest things for a teacher is to know when to keep quiet and when to let go. It is a terrible thing to hold someone back from success, or to insist on sharing credit, or to tie someone to your apron strings. We need to have faith that we have done all we can, and then we need to kick our birds out of the nest.

And I know this is a book about teaching, but I have to say, being a teacher isn't just a job, it's a lifestyle, and civilians can live it, too. Certainly, if you're a classroom teacher, coming up with a way to teach well is a necessity. But teaching is integral to so much of our daily lives that I've found it has infinite practical applications: dating, job interviews, parenting, friendship—you name it.

We are all teachers at various points in life—of our children, our coworkers, and our friends. And I maintain that any good teacher is simultaneously a good student. We learn, ideally, every single day—from those around us, from books, from art and newspapers and our experiences. For me, learning is the only reason to wake up in the morning. If we live life well, we are learning and teaching all the time. If you're not curious about the world around you, you might as well be dead.

I believe it's time to have a national conversation about what makes for a good teacher. In this book, I will take you through my daily life as I look for opportunities to talk about how my T.E.A.C.H. philosophy plays out IRL ("in real life," an acronym I just learned!). Please come along as I draw inspiration from every corner of my life—jury duty, fashion shows, trips on the subway, dinner parties, and, of course, backstage these last thirteen seasons of *Project Runway*. I hope this exercise will remind us to put all our interactions to the T.E.A.C.H. test so that by the end we all become better at teaching and learning—in other words, better at life! Throughout this book I will also share some of the things people have told me about their favorite teachers so that we may all learn from these excellent examples.

I

TRUTH TELLING

ONE OF THE GREATEST gifts our teachers can give us is honesty. We need to hear what our teachers see, whether they believe we're doing a fantastic job or screwing up royally. This is the first stage of a workroom critique: "Here's what I see." Perhaps I see something Kate Middleton would wear. Perhaps it looks to me like something one might wear to take out the trash. I need to let the designer know what I'm seeing, and then to give them an opportunity to tell me what they are going for. This can be awkward. It can be like turning a bright light on in a dark room.

One thing we all need help with is learning how to stomach disapproval and disappointment. Teachers need to make you stronger so you can weather the heartaches to come post-classroom. This is one of several reasons why I am suspicious of those who brag about being "self-taught." In my experience, self-taught designers have nervous breakdowns in high-pressure situations like *Project Runway*. If you haven't been ripped apart in classroom critiques, how will you be strong enough to survive in the lion cage that is the fashion world? I always say what I think. I don't mind that it gets me in trouble. In this chapter, I will explore some of the moments in my life when I realized the value of telling the truth at all costs.

"Throughout my childhood, I was always compared to my brother in terms of 'smarts' and found lacking. I was a classic underachiever. My sixth grade teacher, Miss Jackson, sat me down one day and said to me, 'This work is good enough. However, it is not good enough for *you*.' She really motivated me to think about my strengths. Now every single day I try to push my students just a bit above what they think they can accomplish."

—KIM, COLLEGE PROFESSOR, OREGON

LIFE AS A NEW TEACHER

When I was a classroom teacher, the first day of class was so important to me. There is so much to be said about that first day. We're making a first impression and so are the students. I'd like to think that I'm dispelling their preconceptions and that they are more alert and they're thinking, *Oh! This is engaging!* You want them to know you care about them.

In fact, if someone was absent on that first day, I often told him or her to go ahead and withdraw. That first class was about learning the basics: who they are, who I am, and my rules and expectations. One expectation I always wanted to extinguish was that just showing up to every class meant "I get a B or a C." Showing up is the smallest expectation I had for any of them.

Key to first impressions is, as we all know, what you wear. That goes for both teachers and students. As a teacher, I felt stronger and more in control if I looked professional. Even in my junior days of teaching, I always wore a tie. It might be a knit tie, and I might have worn jeans with it, but a tie denotes effort. I wanted to feel in command, and dressing up helped me do that.

Also key for teachers looking to make a good first impression is to look around the room at the start of every class and fully engage with the students. Opening the class with "How are you?" is a sensational idea, and so simple. In any group, you don't walk in and start to talk. You shouldn't do that in a classroom, either.

I would ask everyone in the class to say their name and something about themselves, and then I would make notes on the roster. I found the students felt more invested if they introduced themselves rather than just saying, "Here!" They had a responsibility to show up and participate and contribute to the chemistry of the class.

"You're all on an even playing field," I told my students in my opening remarks. "You will distinguish yourself up or down from this point forward. Just being here, that's not enough. You have to fully embrace these assignments and do them exceptionally well. You can't be a cipher. Just because you're present doesn't mean you'll get a good grade."

At the end of every class, I would wait until everyone was gone and the next class was coming in, and then I would think, *Now I can go.* Maybe no one would come up to me after class for weeks on end, but I still never rushed out. Whether or not they took advantage all semester of my availability, I wanted them to know that if they did need me, I was there to hear what they had to say.

Every year a couple of students would approach me on that first day and tell me they didn't belong in this class because they had experienced the course's content before and were too advanced. I always said the same thing to them: "For the next four weeks we have an add/drop period. If you show during that time that you are capable of higher-level work, we'll advance you to the next level." Did it ever happen? Never.

That said, at Parsons you are required to attend classes. You were only permitted two absences, period. The classroom experience is why you're there. "I have a doctor's note," a student might say. "It doesn't matter," I would reply. "You've missed this experience. You have four absences. You need to withdraw, or you need to take a leave of absence. You're not going to pass this class. Period."

I would make it clear that this class was about nurturing everyone . . . up to a point.

I would give the students explicit instructions in writing via an extensive syllabus. There always needs to be a syllabus. Teachers who resist having one make me nervous. When I was a department chair, I hosted a syllabus workshop and still found teachers hesitant to commit their teaching philosophies to paper. They were paranoid about sharing. But we needed consistency.

When I handed out my course syllabi, I would make the students sign a document saying they'd received and, most important, read it. This may sound obnoxious, but it was sadly necessary. Two-thirds of the way through the semester, I would invariably hear, "You never told us that!" And I then would take out the syllabus and show them that they had signed something saying otherwise.

One thing I learned in the course of my teaching career was to never judge anyone on that first day. When I started out, I was smug about having the students' characters all figured out at first glance. *Oh, that one seems smart!* or *This one seems not so bright!* But students often—I would say, usually—surprise you. As a young teacher, I misjudged so often that ultimately I stopped judging altogether. It was about reducing my level of frustration. To keep myself from ever uttering the words, "I thought you had such promise," I maintained a mantra of, "Let's wait and see."

Often the really articulate, highly participatory students were all talk. To them I often heard myself saying, "You said you could do it. Now where is it?" If we'd only had one meeting, I would have left impressed, but by week three, I would be underwhelmed. My advice to them was, "Stop talking so much and get to work." To those who initially struck me as weak but who turned out to be brilliant, I said: "Learn how to make a better first impression. Learn how to show off a little."

There's no substitute for experience. I have the greatest respect for new teachers—their enthusiasm, their eagerness to have a great relationship with their students and to help them learn. At the same time, veteran teachers are great beneficiaries of trial and error. Mistakes are so valuable, providing you learn from them. One of the worst things for a teacher is to be stubborn and rigid.

When I began teaching, I erred on being overly kind and generous in my assessment of the students' work. I realized by midterm that it wasn't doing them any favors. What I was really doing was lowering the bar of my expectation to where the students actually were. The trouble with that is, they'll stay there. If the teacher's expectations are higher than what the students can achieve, they'll keep pushing themselves. It's like running a marathon alone: You can't gauge where you are. And so, as I became a more seasoned teacher, I resolved to keep the bar higher.

"My favorite teacher was 'Doc' John Anderson, my political science teacher at Edison High School. I was taken seriously as a school athlete, but no teacher until Doc took me seriously. He paid attention to what I said in class. He showed an interest in me. He uncovered the 'real' Karen. I began to be recognized as a smart kid, not a jock. He meant the world to me. When you are struggling to find yourself, having someone really listen is very important. I graduated with a B.S. in Criminal Justice. I was the first person in my family to get a college degree. Doc gave me the confidence to just go do it. I miss that little guy."

— KAREN, FOOD BANK WORKER, NEW JERSEY

THE *UNDER THE GUNN* WORKROOM

The three competing mentors on the first season of *Under the Gunn*—Anya, Mondo, and Nick—had radically different styles of teaching. And if you throw me into the mix, there's yet another style. On that topic, I experienced some major envy for the mentors, because they had unlimited access to their designers all day, every day. On *Project Runway* I most certainly do not. I have my workroom rounds, my time checks, announcements, and that's it. I'd love to be present for the model fittings, for instance, but I'm not permitted, because of crew and time constraints. Anyway—envy!

Anya, honestly, I initially saw as a wild card. I didn't know whether she'd be able to focus enough on the designers. Well, as students will, she surprised the hell out of me! She was the keenest listener. She was a prober. She pummeled new designers with questions. She was a truth teller about execution, and she didn't miss a trick.

Also, I observed that even though she is very confident, she has a remarkable ability to check her ego at the door. For her, it was about them. And yet, surprisingly, she doesn't appear to be the most popular with *Project Runway* viewers—at least with the ones who come up to me on the street. Strangers tell me, "That Anya, she doesn't know construction!" But on *Under the Gunn* she impressed me beyond words. What she may have lacked in sewing experience when she was a *Runway* designer herself, she makes up for in understanding style and teaching.

She did have one mentoring problem, though. She sometimes became so involved that she nitpicked. At one point she was sitting on a stool staring back and forth between two of her designers. My head would have exploded if I'd been one of them. I told her: "What you have become is what I always feared I would become if I had free rein with the designers: a relentless, overhanging nag. Get out of the workroom!"

I laid down a mandate for all of the mentors that they had to leave the workroom an hour before I called time. Because if they're in there when the clock is running down, all they do is bark orders like, "Hurry up! What about the collar? The sleeve isn't done!" And the designers stay in a state of nonstop panic that is not constructive.

Mondo was a wonderful mentor in many ways. He liked quirkiness in his designers and he gave them room to take chances. And yet, there were times I wished I could shove Mondo out of the way and weigh in myself. He worked from two polarities. One was to give almost no critical feedback but only the most glowing encouragement: "You can do it!" The other was to be intensely specific in telling them what he believed they should do. He needed to strike some happy medium. For the beach challenge, Mondo took palm fronds and placed them under a sheer material and he said to Michelle Überreste, "Look, it's your own textile." Michelle took his suggestion, but the palm-frond textile wasn't her own idea, and she never seemed to fully commit to it. In the end, she was sent home for that design.

"Why aren't you being more diligent truth tellers?" I often asked the mentors. "You know from your own experience when something is impossible! If you don't believe they can pull it off in the allotted time, it is your job to tell them." The issue on one garment by someone on Mondo's team was seam allowance. Mondo didn't express his concern at the time. "I didn't want to make her feel bad," he said when I asked him about it. "Well," I said. "Now she feels bad, because she's on the bottom."

As a mentor you have to say to yourself: Who gives a damn what *I* would do? I'm not the designer here. I'm the teacher. What do *they* want to do, and how can I help them realize the most they can of their potential at this moment, with what they have to work with?

I expected Nick to shine, because he has a lot of classroom experience. I recruited him for the show directly. He was hesitant, but I was very aggressive. I said he'd be great at it. As it turned out, the show was harder for him than either he or I expected. And it caused me to reflect upon my own transition from teacher to mentor, now more than ten years ago.

Teachers and mentors have a common goal: they help students grow into the people they are meant to be. And yet there is a significant difference between being a mentor and being a teacher. As a teacher, I could tell my students what I wanted them to do. As a mentor, that's inappropriate. That's the divide for me. Mentors help their mentees achieve a vision, whatever that vision is. Teachers guide their students toward certain things. Learning to be a mentor after twenty-nine years of being a teacher wasn't a snap for me the way some people assumed it would be. There was a learning curve.

Season 1, Episode 1 of *Project Runway*, I was in the sewing room, sitting at a sewing station, threading a bobbin (a spool on which thread is wound).

"Tim," a producer called to me, "may I see you in the hall-way for a minute, please?"

I met her in the hallway.

"What are you doing?" she asked.

"I'm threading a bobbin," I replied.

"Why?" she asked.

"The designer was having trouble with it," I said. "I was helping her."

"Please don't help the designers," the producer said. "If you thread the bobbin for this designer, you have to thread the bobbin for all of them. Do you want to thread all the bobbins for all the designers for the rest of the show? It's a fairness issue. It has to be all the bobbins, or none of the bobbins."

"Okay," I said. "It's none of the bobbins."

And thank god I made that decision, or right now instead of writing this book I would still be sitting there, threading bob-bins.

Nick was a born bobbin threader, and it made the adjust-ment on the show more difficult for him. There were ways in which he excelled. He brought a vast amount of knowledge to the process. He knew techniques and historical references. And he was very supportive. Actually, that was his Achilles' heel: he was *too* supportive. He never allowed the designer to speak. He filibustered. When I saw him urging his four design-ers to turn out four almost identical red-carpet dresses, I told him he needed to stop giving them ideas altogether.

Because he always had ideas for them, Nick's group became far too dependent. At one point Natalia yells, "Hey

Nick! How's my model's hair?" Nick says, "I'll check!" I went out and found him and said, "Nick, you go back in there and tell Natalia, 'I don't know. You go see what you think.'

"You can't do demos," I said. "This isn't a classroom lesson in topstitching in which you say, 'Watch my hands and then you do it.' It's neither fair nor appropriate." He nodded and stopped for a while, and then he kept backsliding! I would find him in the workroom sketching designs or draping clothes, and I would yell, "Out!"

The problem with doing the work for your mentees, or your students, is that they don't learn, yes, but also that you steamroll over their eccentricities when you should be helping them be seen. It's your job to encourage each person's uniqueness, not stamp it out. No two people need the exact same thing from you as a mentor.

That goes for style, and it also goes for temperament. A shy young woman who has grown up being told not to brag would need help building up the courage to take a risk. A brash, arrogant young man who has always had his way would need help putting his ego in check so that he can learn to cooperate. We all have strengths and we all have things we need to work on.

On the show, judge Jen Rade gave piercing—and reliably excellent—critical feedback. During breaks she'd tell me she was worried she'd been too blunt. "Uh! I'm such a bitch!" she told me one day.

"You're not a bitch!" I told her. "I would have already bitch-slapped you if you were! You're never *mean*. You're a truth teller. Also, you're not so politically correct and plain vanilla that nothing's getting through." As long as the goal is to improve the work rather than to crush dreams, there is value in honest criticism, even if it's tough.

I wanted the mentors to help their mentees handle negative critiques. It's not easy to keep it together when your work is being mocked. But it's one of the most valuable lessons we can learn. I wanted the designers to stand up for themselves. "Don't agree with the judges if they say you made a bad decision!" I urged them. "Spin it. Say, 'I took a risk! I knew you'd love it or hate it. You hate it. I get it. I'll learn from that.' Fight back! Tell them what it is in the work that you want them to see and appreciate." When you stand up for your work, that's an attitude anyone can respect.

I do recognize that standing up to criticism can be hard. One of the most challenging parts of both teaching and learning is taking that ego blow, recovering, and staying strong. Teachers and students both have to do this all day long. It's a lesson Nick learned in the course of the show. I'd noticed that he seemed very nervous, sometimes even manic. I would just take his hand and squeeze it, as if to say *stop*. "This should be old hat for you," I told him. "You have extensive experience both on TV and in the classroom. Why do you seem so jumpy?"

When we were doing promotions for the show, Nick finally opened up. He was talking to David Hillman, the executive from Lifetime in charge of our show, and I was in the same room. It was hard not to listen. David asked Nick, "How's it going?" This was in the heat of my frustration with Nick's micromanagement.

"Oh, I'm terrified," he said.

My ears perked up.

"You've taught for ten years," David said. "Why would you be worried?"

"It's not about the mentoring," he said. "It's about me. I'm afraid the show will ruin my reputation. I think I could look bad."

"You will look bad," I said, interrupting, "if you don't start following these designers rather than leading them! You need to let it be clear that it is the designers' work. This is about them. It's not about you." I don't usually butt in like that, but I cared too much about him and about the show to sit idly by.

Teachers can't let their egos get in the way of doing what needs to be done for whomever they're charged with guiding. Nick wanted his designers' work to be as great as it could be from his point of departure and feared that if their work was subpar, it would ruin *his* reputation. In other words, his ego was far too involved. He saw no other choice but to control every detail.

"You are having the opposite impact of what you want to have," I said. "Micromanaging is ensuring they will not respond well to you. And you need to let go of this idea that what they do is on you. Unless you're making the work, you're not responsible for it."

Going into the workroom one day, I gave him a challenge to speak as little as humanly possible. "Don't you want to learn what this person's doing?" I said. "Make that your goal. Don't give advice. Just listen. Don't tell the designers what to do. You seem to want to fill the silent void with your voice because you're uncomfortable. Let it breathe. Whatever you're thinking you want to tell your designer, ask about it instead. Say, 'What do you think about this neckline? What do you think about the proportion of the skirt and the top?' Pummel the designer with questions."

Well, he did it. He went into the workroom and through great effort, he managed to just stand there, listening. Sometimes he asked, "What do you think?" The designer talked and talked and eventually saw what we were all seeing that needed fixing.

Nick walked out of the workroom a changed man. He'd had an epiphany. He didn't have to exhaust himself. He could just be a steadying, truth-telling presence, and that was enough. That was *more* than enough.

Another issue: Nick is like a lot of teachers—he wants to be a pal. That is a natural instinct, but not a good one. Once the grades are in, if you want to become best friends with a former student, by all means go for it. But during the term, you may not go there. You lose your critical objectivity. You alienate other students, who will resent your playing favorites. And you stop thinking of them as students who need your help and start thinking about them as buddies. As long as you're their teacher, it's not their feelings you should be concerning yourself with; it's their work!

Nick did what I told him. Sure enough, he learned that each designer sees exactly what he sees. He didn't have to say a word except, "I see that, too." It was a huge relief. This burden was lifted. Nick turned to me and said, "Wow, it works!" Even the line producer came running to us and said, "I can't believe that just happened."

There were times he backslid and let his interior micromanager get the better of him, but over the course of the season he evolved so much as a mentor. One of his designers, Oscar, won the show, and Nick truly earned his corresponding win.

"Mrs. Ellis (now Mrs. Radie), my seventh-grade English teacher at Hudson Middle School, challenged me to be a better writer through criticism, not just praising my work as previous teachers had. The first time she gave me a critique instead of just a compliment, it hit hard. I looked up to her so much, it felt like a personal attack. But she was right. My writing was good but needed work. I had a terrible habit of using really awful descriptive terms—like, instead of characters having brown eyes, they had 'mahogany' eyes. When I got to college, where I majored in creative writing, I found the most support in workshops from peers who actually critiqued my work instead of just—not to put too fine a point on it—blowing smoke up my ass. That appreciation came from Mrs. Ellis."

—JILL, ACADEMIC LIBRARIAN, OHIO

THE LIFETIME UPFRONTS

Every year, I attend the television Upfronts for Lifetime, the channel on which *Project Runway* and *Under the Gunn* appear. Upfronts are a network's annual presentation of its upcoming shows, and basically explain to advertisers why their shows deserve the advertisers' investment. That's different from the annual TCAs (Television Critics Association), when the networks provide more in-depth content about their shows to TV journalists.

This year's Upfronts, held at the Park Avenue Armory, went on for an hour and ten minutes. A&E Networks has six channels now, and they all needed to present their case.

I had a fine time at this year's Upfronts, although I did refuse to do a proposed guest spot about diversity with the crew from *Duck Dynasty*. They were trying to revamp their image, as I gathered, and so we were supposed to sit side by side talking about how wonderful diversity was. Well, to me that sounded like I would be vouching for the *Duck Dynasty* group's moral fiber and enlightenment, and I said I wasn't in a position to do that. In my opinion, whatever their good qualities may be, and

I understand that their show is extraordinarily popular, sensitivity to matters of race and sexuality doesn't appear to be key among their strengths.

Around that time I also participated in a reality-show roundtable with two *Hollywood Reporter* journalists. The vixenish *Duck Dynasty* rep—wearing a dress with a distractingly low neckline—was fending off the journalists' questions about the remarks Phil Robertson had made to *GQ* about, among other things, how there was no racism before the Civil Rights Movement.

She explained that the statement had been taken out of context and offered a convoluted response about how, even though he may have "beliefs" to that effect, he treated all people well.

I was unable to keep quiet and asked whether anyone there was surprised that Phil Robertson made these comments. There was dead silence. People came up to me later and said, "I'm so glad you said that! It's what we all were thinking!" Of course, at the time they'd just been staring at the table. *Thanks for the support*, I thought.

Anyway, back to the Upfronts. Some members of the press came up to speak to me. Several asked me about the Met Gala, the formal benefit at the Metropolitan Museum of Art, which was being held around that time. I told them I don't attend. And to the reporter from the *New York Post* I added: "I'm reminded; it's because of an article in the *Post* that I don't go to the Met Gala!"

I explained that ever since the *Post* quoted me talking about how Anna Wintour (creative director of Condé Nast, editor in chief of *Vogue*, and host of the Met gala) was carried down several flights of stairs by bodyguards at a fashion show, I have been persona non grata. (And why was this such a big deal?

I found it a funny anecdote. I didn't make it up; there were loads of witnesses. And yet, my saying it landed me in the hottest water.)

So, no, I have never received an invite to the Met Gala, and I don't expect to. And that's fine with me. Did you hear that this year, Ms. Wintour raised ticket prices from $15,000 a ticket to $25,000 a ticket? And she asked that all the men wear white tie. That means tails and white bow ties! They don't even make those things anymore, except for costume shops. I certainly don't have white tie in my closet, and I don't know anyone who does.

Hats off to Jay Fielden, editor in chief of *Town & Country* (and formerly *Men's Vogue*), who told the *New York Times*: "I think there is something great about trying to encourage a love of formality and injecting that into the pop-culture bloodstream, where so much suffers from the opposite. But I'm not sure where you'd go to find tails. And if I don't know where to get it, who in hell does?"[1]

While we're on the subject of Anna Wintour, let's gossip some more, as I have nothing to lose. Recently I was on a flight from New York to Los Angeles. A flight attendant came over to chat with me, and then she said, "Is that Anna Wintour over there?" pointing across the aisle. I looked.

"Yes, it is," I said.

"Do you think I could say hello?" she asked.

"Of course!" I said, thinking, who can't muster a *hello*?

Well, this lovely young woman goes up to her and begins to say something, and I see Wintour raise her hand ever so slightly on her armrest, at which point a huge man, who I presume to have been a bodyguard, stands up between them and says, "Ms. Wintour does not wish to be disturbed."

Well, I understand not always wanting to have a long conversation on a plane, but this flight attendant merely wanted to say, "So nice to have you on board," and the iron door came clanging down.

Whenever I tell such stories, people say, "Don't you think you should be more careful about what you say? Don't you think you'll become a social pariah?"

To which I say: "From your lips to God's ears. I go out far too much as it is."

"Mr. Rothman, my third grade teacher, went above and beyond. I had been struggling since I started in school, labeled the dumb kid. I had just given up. Mr. Rothman called my parents one evening to have a private discussion. He made it clear that something was very wrong. He recommended out-of-school testing, which my parents got for me. I was diagnosed with an auditory processing disorder, which explained why someone could be talking to me and I would hear something totally wrong, or hear a conversation across the room louder than the one I was having. His single phone call saved me. I'm sure I would have dropped out in frustration if I had ever made it to high school. Instead, I made it to college and graduated with full honors and was on the dean's list every term. I went on to become a teacher. I still struggle with my disorder, but I know what it is and how to deal with it, all thanks to that one phone call from Mr. Rothman."

—ALEXIS, STAY-AT-HOME MOM, PENNSYLVANIA

CLASSROOM CRITIQUES

A big part of design classes is the critique, in which each student's work is presented for discussion. This is essentially what I do when I make the workroom rounds on *Project Runway*.

The first rule I have is do no harm—deal with the students or designers wherever they are in the moment when you encounter them. That often means starting off by biting your tongue. When you're in a mentor-teacher position, there are times when you need to keep quiet. The one big point I kept bringing back to the *Under the Gunn* mentors was this: it's of no use to you or to the designers to talk to them about things they can't change. It's distracting and unhelpful. When the *Project Runway* or *Under the Gunn* judges make statements like, "You should have used red for this garment, not green," it's completely unhelpful. The designer didn't purchase red at Mood, so it wasn't an option. An information-gathering approach would be to ask, "Help me understand why you chose green for this garment." There, that's not so difficult, is it?

When it comes to teaching, I don't believe in hypothetically perfect circumstances. I never tell the *Project Runway* designers what fabric they should have chosen, or what they should have done with the past three hours, any more than I would tell them they should be taller. You have to meet people where they are. The questions to keep in the forefront are: *What skills do you have? What materials do you have on hand? What is the best thing you can do with them?* It's my job to help the designers ask themselves those questions and come up with answers that help them along.

The time to comment on fabric, for example, is before the trip to Mood. That is the moment in which to say: "You know you don't do well with silk. We're about to go to Mood. Don't even go to the silk aisle." But in the construction stage, that is not a productive conversation to have. That's the point at which you say: "We're at the end of the fourth quarter. Let's figure out how to play this."

At one point during a workroom session, Nick said, "If you had five more hours, you could . . ."

We don't! Why say that? If you had all the time in the world, sure, you could do a Gaultier-style beaded cheetah on the front of a dress that involves 1,030 hours of meticulous beadwork. On *Project Runway* we have ten hours and maybe $200, so let's start from there.

That's true in every area of life. If we had infinite resources, we could all become presidents and CEOs and zillionaires. But we have to figure out what we have to work with and do the best we can with that.

When I was leading critiques in fashion school, I was shocked by how unwilling students often were to tell one another the truth. You'd get pablum-y pandering. "It's really cute," they would say. I thought they would be the truth tellers.

Nope. It was that classic playground thing: they were afraid of retribution.

My instruction to them was: If you're having a positive response, use particulars. Talk about what it is. And then I had to discipline them to do it. They would say, "What a fantastic concept! What great work!"

"Ms. Leyendecker made physics fun and accessible to me, a student who seriously lacked science knowledge. She showed us how physics applied to everyday things. Even though I was a B and C student in eleventh grade, I signed up for college-level physics in twelfth grade just because she was teaching it. From her I learned not only what makes a plane fly, but also to never underestimate myself."
—MELISSA, GRADUATE STUDENT, TEXAS

"Why?" I would ask. They didn't know what to say. Often what they were looking at was very limited. And so I prohibited the phrase "I like it because," or "I don't like it because." The more productive question was: "What do you see? Objectively, what are you looking at? Tell me."

When I took over as chair of the fashion program, I was horrified that only the faculty member was allowed to speak in a critique. I'm talking about perfectly nurturing teachers. But the rule was that there would be no call of hands for students to contribute their feedback. It was embedded in the department's culture. That was alarming to me. When I was teaching, I was the least important person in the room as far as I was concerned—my students' points of view mattered most. I wanted to learn who they were and teach them to respect one another's perspectives.

I would start off by saying something like, "I am having trouble understanding how this work solves the problem at hand. Here are some things about the work that I appreciate: X, Y, Z. But I see these virtues independent of the problem we're solving."

I go back to the first challenge of *Runway*'s Season 12: the parachute challenge. If I had not had a brand-new role on the show—presenting the top three and bottom three looks to the judges and sharing their back stories— Miranda Levy, who hardly used the parachute material, would have won! I warned her in the workroom that the parachute material had to dominate and that, accordingly, she had to use more of it. I told the judges, "It may be very pretty, but if she were my student, she would have received an F. She didn't do the assignment." I said, "If you let her win, you send the message that you don't have to follow the rules. You can ignore the parameters of the challenge and still win. What a terrible precedent." If it's your job to bake a cake, and you build a chair, then it doesn't matter how fantastic that chair is, you haven't done your job.

Often students would become defensive and shut down. They frequently would tell me some variation of the following: "The work speaks for itself!" My response: "But it's not speaking to me, so speak for it! Pretend I'm an editor for the *New York Times* and you want me to assign a story about you. Help me understand why this work is the way it is and why it's important and new."

Young designers often have trouble learning to sell their

vision to others. This is why being surrounded by peers going through the same struggle is so valuable. They can help one another figure out how to do it. One student may not be able to see what makes her own work special, but she will be able to tell her friend, "I love your work! It's like outdoorsy clothes for socialites!" or "You have such an edgy sensibility, but your clothes are still very quiet. They're like shy punk-rock clothes!" Those students who weren't too closed off to hear that kind of advice benefited greatly from it.

It's also key for students making creative work to develop a willingness to share and trust an audience. I have little patience for preciousness. The morning of the judging I would take the *Under the Gunn* mentors into the workroom to talk about where their designers were in the process. Every time, I noticed Oscar would cover his designs with muslin.

"He's concerned about dust," Nick said.

"No, he's not," I said. "I bet this is about protecting his creativity."

One time during an extended critique I asked Oscar to uncover the dress form, and he said, "No, I'm not showing you anything, because I'd rather have it be a surprise on the runway."

"Oh, okay," Nick said.

"No, it's not okay," I said. "There will be no surprises on the runway. We're your safety net."

Sure enough, when we looked at his design, we saw immediately that it was entirely too complicated and would never make sense to the judges. I said, "Keep going with this if you want to, but I think it's a mistake."

In school, there was always a student who would say, "I have to show you this project privately." They would whisper: "I don't want anyone else to see it."

"You don't own your dress designs in this nation," I would say. "You have no protection. Show it."

Grudgingly, the student would unveil the secret special creation. Nine times out of ten it would be something completely pedestrian, like an A-line skirt.

"What's unique about this?" I would ask.

"The zipper's *in the front*," they would whisper excitedly.

"There's a reason why the zipper is traditionally in the back or on the side," I would respond. "Otherwise it's vulgar."

And you would see them suddenly see this secret thing they've been obsessed with for weeks in a whole new light. "Ohhhh," they would say.

At the *Project Runway* Season 13 auditions, I met a designer in his thirties who had been working on his designs for more than ten years but hadn't started his own label yet. When I asked him why not, he said, "Because I don't want anyone to copy me. I'm waiting until I have the right backing."

"That's a terrible reason," I said. "There is no piracy protection in this country for designers, so anyone can copy you at any time, no matter what your stature in the industry. You can copyright your logo. It's a graphic design. But you can't copyright your clothes. So get out there and show your work!"

I tell all wary designers the same thing: The problem for 99 percent of artists is not being ripped off, but being ignored.

"Mr. Cutting, my high school English teacher, used to make us do loads of really bizarre activities, like creating outfits out of newspaper and acting out scenes we wrote, which had absolutely nothing to do with the curriculum. At the time we loved him, because we thought he never made us do any work. We totally didn't realize he was teaching us loads, but in secret! I went from hating English to loving it!"

—CHARLOTTE, COLLEGE STUDENT, UK

THE ADMISSIONS OFFICE

I had a provocative role on the admissions committee at Parsons. I was always saying to the other members, "Don't just look at the portfolio! Look at the transcript. Where are they from? What school? What's the art department like?" For three or four years, I was on the road all the time to experience the schools. You can't take a kid from a magnet art school and say, "This kid is better than this kid from Anchorage." Yes, the opportunities are greater, so the work is more developed. But if you have a kid from Alaska from a school that's sixty kids K–12 who's making remarkable work, that shows real drive, I'd bet all my money on the kid from Anchorage. I'm not saying the magnet student can't continue to excel. But we can't turn our back on the kid from Anchorage.

Affirmative action is a controversial topic today. As a member of the Parsons admissions committee, I was always in favor of it. We were diligent about offering admission to a very diverse group of people and recruiting applicants who would bring diversity to the school. I lobbied for affirmative action, as I was deeply concerned by the low number of enrollments of Latinas and Latinos and African Americans.

Not only is it important to provide opportunities to mi-
norities and the poor, but by not creating a diverse environment, you are doing a grave disservice to the more privileged
students. It's a critically important life lesson to learn how to
get along with people from all classes and races. I was fairly
sheltered growing up, but when I reached art school, I encountered the most diverse group of people I had been with up to
that point. I found it thrilling. For me, being around people
from all over the country and the social spectrum went hand in
hand with the freeing atmosphere of art school. I felt so lucky
to be there.

The trouble with our efforts to bring diversity to Parsons
was that we didn't have the financial resources to help needier
students enroll. We would offer them admission and they
would turn us down because they couldn't afford it.

To me it seemed grossly unfair. Parsons was the only profit-
able division of the university (New School University, which
has eight divisions, the largest by far being Parsons). Only 9
percent of tuition came back for financial aid. Other divisions
had 48 percent! That was our money! We were the cash cow,
and it was going to other divisions.

"This is repugnant!" I said. "We want financially challenged
African-American students from the Baltimore School for the
Arts! And we can't get them, because we can't offer competitive packages." The NACAC (National Association for College
Admission Counseling) thought of us as stellar in how we
operated with affirmative action, but in my eyes we were a
big failure. We were so diligent in recruitment and admissions
committee work, but we failed miserably when it came to ensuring enrollment.

Anyone whose family could write a check for the full

admission could enroll. And if you were really, really, really poor, there were enough federal and state grants to get you in. But if you were working class, or middle class, you were expected to pay an unrealistic amount of the cost of your education. We ended up being a division with rich students and poor students, and almost no one in the middle. There was nothing to mitigate those two extremes. As an educator, I found that this polarity dramatically diminished the dialogue in the classroom. That troubled me tremendously.

For example, I had the students do shopping reports. They had to go everywhere from Bergdorf's to the Gap to H&M and come back and report on what they were seeing and share information.

One parent called me wanting to know more about this shopping report project because apparently it was causing his daughter to spend a fortune on clothes. "I'm getting these credit card bills for thousands of dollars," he said.

"They don't have to spend a cent," I told him. "They just have to write a report about what they're seeing in stores." She was just pulling a fast one on her rich family.

Another day while we were talking about what was in the stores, a group of students presented this disdain for the Gap: "Who would ever go there?"

One student of mine, Flora Gill, piped up and said, "Where I grew up, the Gap was like Bergdorf's. We had Kmart and Walmart and then we had the temple of high taste, the Gap. People *ooh*ed and *ahh*ed when new clothes came in there, and I did, too. I still like the Gap."

I've never forgotten that. It was humbling for everyone. Flora and her classmate Alexa Adams have had a successful collaboration under the name Ohne Titel. And I think of her every time I look at the Bergdorf Goodman catalog, where you see $1,800 pants and $400 T-shirts. Kanye West's plain white T-shirt for A.P.C. retailed for $120. The only thing dumber than that is the person who would buy it. I say get one from Hanes and give the balance of the money to charity. Or to a promising designer in the form of a Mood gift certificate.

The faculty on the admissions committee often complained about my applicant selection choices, because I was a champion for the underdog. "The rest of you just want the superstars, because they're easy to teach," I told them. It's my philosophy that sometimes our most difficult students can be our favorites, and ultimately the most successful. You bear witness to an evolution. You see it happen. I had faculty come to me and say, "I have the worst class!" I would say, "Don't be a fatalist. Don't be depressed. It should be exciting! Think of the impact you can have if they really are the worst students ever. They have nowhere to go but up!"

I also told faculty members that if they found their students to be boring, which I heard with too much frequency, then they should quit. I would say, "This is the hand you've been dealt. Play it." We're always looking for the best, and the misconception is that that's the person who requires the least attention. I was always most excited by those with the greatest apparent potential and the least resources. Education should be life changing. I would rather pick raw students with tons of potential. Those are the kids I love the most. Having the opportunity to observe their growth is exciting! And for a student who has been stigmatized in the past, just having someone believe in you can be all it takes.

"My favorite teacher was Jim Kessler, my English teacher in my junior and senior years in high school. He taught me to appreciate the written word, how to organize my own thoughts for a writing assignment, and to have fun in the process. What he taught me served me well in college and in my career. And I ended up marrying a teacher!"

—SHANNON, RETIRED SOCIAL WORKER, KENTUCKY

MY FIRST PARSONS FASHION CLASS

I began teaching in the Parsons fashion department in September 2001, a year after I began there. I inherited a class from a teacher named Path Song, who abruptly quit. She lived by the World Trade Center. Her leaving wasn't psychological as much as geographical. Her apartment was destroyed. It was so disruptive, she said she couldn't teach that semester. I inherited her twenty students (in a class of seventy seniors), all of whom had petitioned as juniors to take her class. They were total grumps without her. They loved Path. And I learned why. She brought no discipline to the class. It was all laissez-faire. I became very frustrated and angry. But I decided to hear them out. I asked them what was wrong. They were industrious, serious students. They were challenging the system. And in spite of this new curricular threshold, there were some lingering vestiges of the old regime.

Some aspects of the former curriculum I actually subscribed to, such as expecting a certain volume of work: forty croquis (sketches of work) for a single assignment. Why? In the process of doing forty, you'll make yourself explore areas of your own conceptual development that you wouldn't otherwise. You have to grow with each successive sketch or get bored of your own work. I'd experienced that myself as an art student. These students in my class would say, "If we have ten fabulous ideas, why do we have to give you forty?" I said, "Because I say so!" That was my first strategy, and I wasn't proud of it! They became grumpier and I became more frustrated. Then I said, "Bring in as many as you think you need to represent yourself as a designer. Think of it as showing a collection on a runway. Would you show six? Would you show forty?"

We debated it, because then they were challenging the concept of the fashion show. Gradually, I grew to rather like their spirit. They said, "It's been the same for a hundred years. It should change!" I came to realize that they were right. "You drank the Kool-Aid!" other faculty members said. "No," I said, in the students' defense, "they're unhappy for good reasons."

That six-hour class got me to start thinking outside the box. And it also challenged the last vestige of what was left of the former department. It was about busywork before. *Don't think about what you're doing; just do it.* Everything was by rote. That's not productive. I remember saying to the faculty— every two to three weeks we met as a group—that there was a delusion at work, this notion that just producing volumes and volumes of work would ensure something good would happen. "It's that old theory," I said. "'Give a thousand monkeys a thousand typewriters for a thousand years and one will write *Gone with the Wind*.' Well, it's not true. Maybe you get a *Gone with the Wind*, but even if you do, it will be lost amid a thousand years' worth of babble."

There was a particularly combative student in that class. I stood in support of the challenges he made to the status quo and his rallying cry against tradition for tradition's sake. But I also thought he could be quite petty. When two of his looks were selected for the senior show, he petitioned the department. He wanted to show his entire collection. So he pulled his two looks from the fashion show at the last minute. It screwed up our model lineup. Talk about needing to make it work! His action hurt him, and it hurt other people. I was mad as hell.

Two days later there was a knock at my office door. It was the student. I thought he was going to deliver a mea culpa. No, he wanted a recommendation.

"Don't sit down," I said, not even rising from my desk, which was very unlike me. I always rose and greeted students. "I wouldn't recommend you to walk a dog around the block. You would come back without the dog, the dog would come back without you, or you would come back with a totally different dog. Leave."

REPOSITIONING THE PARSONS FASHION
DESIGN PROGRAM

In August 2000, the dean of Parsons tasked me with repositioning the fashion design program for the twenty first century.
Having run the search for a new chair earlier that year, I knew
the department was in a state of dubious morale. What I didn't
know was that the place was actually hemorrhaging. The program was heralded as being the best of its kind; I was excited to
lead this charge. And then I found out that it was a dressmaking school, not a fashion department. I was devastated by it.
I'd talked about it so enthusiastically in the past. But quickly I
learned it was a sham.

At best, it was a dressmaking school. There was minimal
computer technology, fashion history, or design dialogue. You
watched a faculty member talking about how to improve the
eye shadow in an illustration. "If you add a henna highlight, it
will pop!" NO. We have to talk about the clothes. The students
had no vocabulary for the critical analysis of design content. It
was the teacher talking at them, and the teacher wasn't talking
about design content, either! The faculty never asked, "What
do others think?" They never said, "Present your work. Who's

your customer? What's your price range? Where would this be sold?"

In building a new curriculum in the fashion program, we had to ask: What is the base of learning required in order to lead this industry, not merely get a job, and what are the proficiencies needed? We had six sections of course work at every year level. When the students at any level—with the exception of the spring of senior year—are moved forward to the next semester, the faculty teaching that semester should have confidence that the students know certain material. It's not just course content and classroom experience; it's also vocabulary.

Once I overheard six junior-year teachers fighting over the definition of a dolman sleeve. I found it preposterous, and concerning, that each of these teachers was telling his or her students something different. I said, "I don't care what it is. All I care about is that you, the faculty, share a common definition. All six of you have to agree." As far as I'm concerned, we should all go with Fairchild's excellent dictionary of fashion terms. I bought them each a copy of that book.

"All six of you are Parsons educated," I said. "You're telling me that when you were studying—in other words, since the fifties—there has been no objective definition of terms like this? It's up to the teacher?"

"Yes," they told me.

"Those days are over, people," I said.

It wasn't the last time I encountered such a problem. There's always latitude in your manner and your style and your thoughts. I celebrate that. That's what makes the experience in the classroom so special. But the teacher is responsible for content and the delivery of that content. And then there's pedagogy. How is the information delivered? And what is the student's engagement? I'd like to think the teacher is an orchestra conductor. The students are the instruments. It's about making music.

When I went to South Asia, I was shocked to learn that in classes teachers lecture *at* the students. Classes are lecture style. You're spoken at. My students from South Asia would say, "I don't talk." I said, "You must talk!" It was key to their grades. You can't sit and be a cipher. A lot of their apprehension was fear based. It helped me understand how important it is to have a healthy classroom environment, where you feel comfortable speaking out, taking risks, saying something potentially provocative. You won't be shouted at. You won't be ridiculed. There may be a discussion, but that's a healthy thing. I was constantly having conversations with teachers about creating a healthy classroom environment.

A warning sign to me was when I could hear teachers shouting. If you're shouting, you're in trouble. You hold the power in your two hands. If you have any moment of disbelief about that, who is giving them a grade? You are. You're in charge. You have all the power. There is no reason to raise your voice. You can be angry. You can express disappointment. But never yell. If you can't handle it, walk out. Walk around the block and then come back. Or walk to one of the advisors or the department chair. They're not just there for students. They're there for you, too.

I also learned that you can't let the students who are achieving at the lower end set the pace. That's what I found at Parsons when I took over the fashion design department. "They're just a bunch of dummies," one of my predecessors said. And dummies were the focus of the curriculum. You had the students who did everything quickly, and they were being treated like dummies, too. There's a responsibility to both constituencies.

The lion's share of how you direct your instruction has to be to the group in the middle.

"A good teacher tries to make learning fun and innovative. My world history teacher, Mrs. Hamilton, would dress up and do voices. A good teacher also gives you advice that you find very useful and true when you get older. My high school math teacher, Mr. Tuttle, always said that the calculator is only as smart as you are. I have found that is true on more than one occasion. But I have to say my parents are my favorite teachers. My dad is a self-made man. I see him get up every day and go to work for ten to eleven hours. My mom also works very hard. They taught me to always strive to reach goals, to depend on myself and work hard."

—MAIA, COLLEGE STUDENT, CALIFORNIA

Some teachers would take that übertalented group and have them help the others. But they can't be studio assistants to you! They have to get something out of the class, too. And it puts them in an awkward position vis-à-vis their peers. The first year chairing the department, all I could do was observe and pummel people with questions. The more I probed, the more horrified I was. Everyone was so infantilized—students by teachers, teachers by the administration.

One of the biggest problems was the Parsons designer critic program. Founded in 1948, the program was the first of its kind in an academic institution. It brought in top-tier designers to oversee senior projects comprised of eight to ten looks each. Claire McCardell and Norman Norell were among those who came in that first year. In 1952, Christian Dior came in as a critic! Can you imagine? It would be like having God come in as a guest speaker.

The looks developed under the direction of the designer critics would be presented at the annual fashion show. Each student would generate one garment per semester. That was their focus: one mere garment per semester. In 2000, when I walked in, I thought of the designer critic program as the jewel in the crown of the department. Soon I realized that it was an anachronism whose time had come and gone.

Yes, it had had a time and a place. That was when this nation was coming into its own as a fashion center after World War II. Fashion design students at that time weren't being taught to think like entrepreneurs. They were taught how to work under a designer to produce a collection. But by the time we reached the late 1980s, the designer critic construct seemed like an anachronism, so dated a concept.

When I was associate dean, prior to being appointed chair of fashion, Donna Karan, an active alumna who served on the board of governors, kept saying to me, "You have to get rid of this [the designer critic program]. It's not good for them." Among the structural issues, in terms of delivering the program, was the unreliable and quixotic schedule of the critics. Eighteen hours a week were devoted to this process. A week!

When I arrived in the department in 2000, I noticed that 50 percent of the entire faculty budget was in the senior year. I made an assumption that these were the more senior people, so that's why most of the budget was there. But it was actually because there were simply more faculty in the senior year. Why? Because the teachers were working on the students' clothes! The students were ill prepared to do the work demanded by the designer critics. The teachers didn't want the department to be embarrassed in front of the critics.

In the jury show three weeks prior to the annual fashion show, we presented the designer critics' collections, consisting of 140 looks, to a group of journalists, fashion editors, and buyers. They voted yes or no on each garment. Everything got in regardless of how the jurors voted. It was a ruse. But the things that received low scores would be redesigned.

"I have two favorite teachers: Mrs. Margaret Badger (third grade) and Mr. Jim Gorman (seventh grade math). Mrs. Badger taught me to wonder and not take things just as they were presented to me. She encouraged me to speak up and not be afraid of my own voice. Mr. Gorman taught me the importance of being civil and courteous to others. He never accepted a 'what?' a 'yeah,' or 'uh-uh.' He required 'excuse me,' 'yes,' or 'no' inside his classroom. Even to this day, twenty-eight years later, I still find myself making sure that I respect people enough to give them a proper, complete answer."

—RHEA, EXECUTIVE ASSISTANT, VIRGINIA

So here's a summary of the designer critic program process. Stage 1: the senior administration hovered as the critics arrived to present the design concept. The students had to do croquis and flat patterns for the critics. There were some twenty illustrations of concepts. The critics would play with them like a deck of cards: ripping them up, saying things like, "Let's do this top with this bottom." No explanation. Just, "Here's what we need to make a collection out of these ten students' drawings." There was never a question of whether the student could complete any specific item. A jacket is difficult to execute, for example, whereas a circle skirt is not.

Stage 2: The selected designs would be executed in muslin. Reviewing the students' work, the critic would talk to him- or herself while cutting away, ignoring the students, and just doing whatever he or she felt like. "Let's do three-quarter sleeves," the critic might say, lopping off cuffs. I felt so bad for the students. They were making lots of meaningful eye contact with me during this process. And keep in mind that this was my first year in the department, the year during which I could merely observe and make notes, tons and tons of notes.

Stage 3: The designer critic's staff would come in with, for example, loads of three-ply cashmere. The students weren't even selecting their own fabrics. Then everyone got ready for the designer critics' visits to see the students' looks in final fabric. But, by way of another infantilizing example, the designer's office would call to say, "She's doing textile research in Milan. She can't be there for ten days." Wouldn't you think if you were on the faculty, you would test your students' deftness at execution? Wouldn't you do exercises with them?

But no. They just sat there and waited for the designer critic return. I could not stand it. I recruited fabulous people to advise me, including the best and brightest in the senior class. "I'm not Donna Karan, Jr.!" one of the students said. "This isn't preparing me for anything but to be that."

That spring I didn't consult anyone on the faculty before going straight to the junior year students with my plan. Usually I was very collaborative. But I felt like the time for that was past. I met with the juniors. I said, "I'm making an assumption.

Most of you came here because you're so eager to participate in the designer critic program."

"Yes!" they said.

"How many of you would be upset if it went away?" I asked.

There was dead silence. Finally, a student asked, "What will we do instead?"

"Instead," I continued, "you will design and execute a collection that is your point of view as a designer. It will be a minimum of five to seven looks." They leaped to their feet and started cheering.

"How many of you are terrified?" I asked.

Two people put their hands up.

"All of you should have a hand raised," I said. "You are completely unprepared for this challenge. The responsible thing for me to do would be to fix the sophomore year first, then junior, then senior, but I can't subject you to this program. I'd rather raise the bar and have you stretch to reach it."

In any event, the students were on board. Then I had to work on the faculty. They said, "The students can't do this!" I said, "If you treat them like dummies, they will probably meet those expectations."

I said faculty members weren't allowed to make the students' clothes anymore. Three years of curriculum needed to be rewritten. And we had to completely reconstruct the pedagogy. It had been: they're dummies. We tell them what to do. Now faculty had to engage students differently. We had to make their voices important. This was about *them*. "We can't let them do just anything," the faculty said.

"Why not?" I asked.

They explained to me that the department subscribed to the aesthetics of the Calvin Kleins and Donna Karans and Ralph Laurens.

"Well," I said, "from this point forward, if the student wants to be the next Dolce and Gabbana or Jean Paul Gaultier, that's what we're going to help them be."

To me, it seemed necessary, but it started a war. I was persona non grata in the New York fashion community. The head of the Parsons Los Angeles sister program, the Otis College of Art and Design, made it clear to me that she didn't approve of my changes. I had what I thought was a polite relationship with her, but it went sour.

"Dr. Howard Hendricks from Dallas Theological Seminary taught me to take the time to observe the world. He taught me that creativity is essential to teaching. He said it was sinful to bore your students. And he loved life. From him I learned that it's important to take the time to know your students. Don't prejudge them, and don't ever give up on them!"

—KARIN, CHILDREN'S PASTOR, CALIFORNIA

Later that month, I had a 911 call from the dean's office. I bolted to the subway and went running into his office. Lo and behold, there were six former designer critics all facing me. Randy Swearer, the dean, said, "I asked Tim to come here because I wanted him to hear me tell you, this is an experiment. I'm betting on the success of this. It may fail, in which case we'll hope that you will return. But this is a new threshold for us. We're going to do it."

I was so disarmed. One of the critics was the then-president of the CFDA (Council of Fashion Designers of America), Stan Herman, and he was the maddest. He was a powerful guy. But he was a uniform designer. My impression was that he needed us to validate him as an artist in spite of his utilitarian work.

After every designer-critic-driven fashion show, the press would always exalt: the Badgley Mischka collection! The Marc Jacobs collection! Each collection was presented with the name of the critic, never mentioning the students.

The first year of the new curriculum, the students had seven hundred looks for the jury show. That's the expected outcome of having seventy seniors each create a collection, as compared to one look a semester. But we weren't going to parade seven hundred looks up and down the runway; it would have gone on for days. Over the course of three days we presented three groups of roughly twenty-five students each. We had mannequins. We gave each student his or her own 10 x 10 square-foot piece of the auditorium in which to display the collections. They could do something to the 10 x 10 environment if they wanted. The jury could come in and vote and leave. I found it interesting that most of the jurors came all three days and spent a lot of time looking around.

At the end of the process, I sat with the senior-year faculty and looked over the ballots. I made decisions based on the votes.

"Isn't it all going to be shown?" one of the teachers asked.

"Seven hundred looks?!" I asked. "No."

The ballots determined that out of these seventy collections, twelve needed to be shown in their entirety. Fourteen students—20 percent of the class—weren't to be shown at all. The remaining forty-four students had one, two, or three pieces in the show. All hell broke loose. The screaming mass, interestingly enough, wasn't those fourteen rejected people. There was grumpiness among them, surely, but it was the people with only one to three looks who revolted.

"It's unfair!" they said. "We're outraged!" I told them they could pull their work out in protest if they so chose, adding that they needed to make that decision right away so we could plan for it.

Students—and some members of the faculty—signed a petition demanding my firing and presented it to the dean. Stan Herman said that the work lacked "the lush, rich, high-end luxury that used to be Parsons. And the textiles! What a load of crap."

"Stan, when you were a designer critic, you guided the textile decisions of your students," I said. "Your absence has exposed a major deficiency in the department's curriculum. These students need to know what all the textile possibilities are—what they feel like, what they'll do. It's very apparent that they don't know any of it. And that's changing."

"It's been nice knowing you," he said in a huff.

Then the selected students' work was shown. Well, after the show, the audience stood and cheered. They screamed. Nothing like it has ever happened at a show I've been to. They loved it.

The buyer for Barneys, Julie Gilhart, bought the entire Proenza Schouler boys' collection right off the runway.

Even Stan had a change of heart. He came up, threw his arms around me, and said, "Never go back. I never dreamed the students were capable of this."

Furthermore, the press was beyond anything that the annual fashion show had ever received. And the journalists talked about the students' work, not the party. I don't know when I've ever felt quite as proud.

The next year I decided we would only show full collections; none of these one-offs from a larger body of work. Thanks to the work of our diligent jury of selection, we chose twenty-four out of seventy collections. Those rejected students went crazy.

And they rebelled. As was the case with the preceding class, they wrote a petition that called for my dismissal, but instead of presenting it to the dean, they took it directly to the university president. Furthermore, they went to *Women's Wear Daily*. Eric Wilson, the thoughtful *WWD* reporter with whom they spoke, called and asked me for my side of the story. The story was on the cover of *WWD* on the very day of the show.

The big, splashy runway gala is in the evening. Earlier in the day, we have a show for the Parsons community. At that daytime show, a group of hostile seniors stormed the runway in protest wearing T-shirts bearing my face with a big X through it. They also put a black rabbit in my office. Apparently it's an Eastern European threat of some kind. Someone told me it was considered a curse. Well, that bunny was hard to catch. It was quite speedy. The head of maintenance, Pasquale, finally captured it and asked the student group what they wanted him to do with it.

"We certainly won't touch it!" they said. "It's a curse!" Pasquale took that to mean that he could do whatever he wanted with the animal, and so he took it to a farm in New Jersey, where it lived happily ever after. The rabbit actually came out ahead. I was left back in New York City, loathed.

After the daytime show, there was much discussion with the powers that be about the evening presentation: Should there be security, for example, in case the students acted out again? I said, "If it's going to happen, let it happen. We'll survive. Besides, the press already has the story."

Frankly, I was afraid that the presence of security might serve to incite the group rather than cause them to extinguish their protest. I wanted to carry on and think positively. At evening's end, all was well. Whew!

My firm belief was that there was too much focus on that

damn show. We had to put on some form of show, because it was the most visible event the school presented. More important, from the administration's perspective, it was the centerpiece of the fund-raising for the entire institution. But for the students' sake, department traditions needed to be challenged. And so, the following year I devised a new senior presentation that would offer some counterpoint to the senior fashion show.

Each student would have three models and as many mannequins as they needed. The point of the models was to see those three looks move and walk. The students would have ten minutes to present their work before a panel of designers, editors, buyers, and curators. More outrage, this time over the ten-minute time limit. I heard variations on: "We've been at this school for four years and you expect us to cram all that we've learned and done into ten minutes?!"

In response to this new Sturm und Drang, I assembled the senior students and faculty. "You should want to present your work. Ten minutes is a short film," I said, "but it's a long commercial. This is a commercial for you."

Well, over time the faculty worked to get the students into shape for these little commercials, and the caliber of work and presentation became better and better. Students even had stores buying their work as a result of these meetings. This new presentation gave students the opportunity to personally engage with the panel rather than just having their work looked at, as was the case with the jury show. It was an audition and a job interview in one. Eventually, this presentation became the focal point of the senior experience, and the fashion show took second place, drifting into the back of people's minds. I was very happy about that. My only regret, looking back, is that I never got one of those T-shirts with the image of my crossed-out face.

The repositioning of the curriculum and teaching pedagogy in the Parsons fashion program is hands-down the professional work of which I am most proud. Buoyed by a few successes early on in the process, I totally underestimated how tremendously difficult and challenging it would be to change an academic culture. It was so critically important for me to stay the course, rather than retreat to the status quo and suffer defeat. My ability to see it through had everything to do with my belief system; that is, whatever the cost, a school must constantly improve for its students. Individuals and groups will adjust. Would I have the courage and energy to do that same work today? Never!

"I came from a poor household. My mother made me a fur coat out of an old fur she had gotten from a charity. I was so proud of that coat and it was warm for the long, cold walk to school during winters in Rhode Island. One teacher told me it looked like a run-over bear. Very hurtful. At the other end of the spectrum was Mrs. Ripley, a kind, gentle woman who read stories to us in the fourth grade and treated everyone with respect. She opened up the world of reading and storytelling to me. She allowed us to relax— and she even smelled good!"

—MARTHA, SOFTWARE EDUCATOR, NEW YORK

THE COOPER HEWITT NATIONAL
DESIGN MUSEUM TEEN FAIR

I was asked to be a guest critic for a high school program run by the Cooper Hewitt National Design Museum. This particular group of students was studying fashion design. I arrived bright and eager. Enthusiastic faces were in abundance. Then I looked at the work. It was bizarre.

"What do you think?" the students and teacher asked me.

I invoked my now-familiar phrase before weighing in. "Talk to me," I said.

They all just smiled and glistened with pride in their work.

"Was there a theme?" I asked. "Was there a problem to be solved? What was the point of departure for this work?"

"We're designing clothes for people who live on the moon!" a student said brightly.

"Um, okay," I responded. "Tell me about these looks."

Well, it was all so preposterous, frankly. These designs were costumes at best.

Every time I asked a question, such as, "Why are there wings?" or "Why did you choose this fabric?" the students—

and teacher—responded to my observations and comments with the refrain: "It's for the moon!"

What a big pile of excuses. We don't know what it's like getting dressed on the moon! When those are the fuzzy parameters, everything is possible and there's no helpful criteria for assessment.

"What is this pleat for?"

"She's going to a party—on the moon." Or "She works in an art gallery—on the moon."

"No more parties!" I finally said. "No more art gallery assistants!" And to myself I said, *No more moon!*

After the critique, which I soft-pedaled because of the students' age, I took the teacher aside and said, "I have a problem with this assignment. When you have them design for the moon, there's no tangible point of departure. There are no variables available to evaluate how appropriately or inappropriately the students addressed the problem to be solved. You had garments with thirty-foot wings. What is this, Leonardo da Vinci? If that were the intended inspiration, okay, but absent that specific directive, these clothes were ridiculous."

"Well," the teacher said defensively, "I don't want them to do boring stuff."

"Those are the only options—boring or the moon? Making interesting work for this planet is the most important challenge for a young designer," I said. "It's easy to make something absurd. But how do you create clothes that can navigate the real world without being boring? That's hard." I told the head of the program that the students' experience in the course seemed like a waste of time. She took great offense, but I stand by that assessment.

I always think of what my dear friend Grace Mirabella,

former editor in chief of *Vogue*, says about gimmicky clothes. She was a guest speaker in my classes every semester that I taught in the fashion program, because I loved her message to the students.

"You are the future of this industry," Grace would say. "You have a huge responsibility to it and to yourselves. And I have two pieces of advice: don't design dumb clothes and don't make jokes."

The students would all look at one another quizzically.

"Dumb clothes: the world doesn't need you to design a T-shirt," she went on. "There are more than enough of them out there. Jokes: those things that walk the runway during Paris Couture Week. It's easy to make a float in a parade. It's hard to design for that space in the middle: innovative, beautiful, and believable clothes. It's very hard! Don't design dumb clothes and don't make jokes when you can make something beautiful."

God bless you, Grace Mirabella.

"I went to private school and was on the path to pursuing the liberal arts, as I loved history and English. But my favorite teacher was Sister Kenneth Marie, who taught the sciences. She was fantastic at engaging all of us in biology, chemistry, and physiology. She was extremely creative in her teaching, using humor and real-life analogies. She changed the path of my life, and so much of what I learned from her has stuck with me to this day. I'm sixty-one, so that's a long time!"

—JOANNA, DIRECTOR, NEW JERSEY

THE FACULTY LOUNGE

As chair of the School of Fashion at Parsons, I had a talk with the faculty about how they presented themselves. This was a talk that I never in my wildest dreams ever imagined needing to have. These are individuals who teach fashion, I thought, so their manner of dress and appropriateness should be second nature. Wrong.

One of the teachers actually wore pajama pants to class—with *soccer balls* on them. What kind of message does that send to young people? It says that you don't care, and they don't need to care, either. I can see young people across America saying, "Mom, I'm going to school today in my pajamas. My teacher does!" That's appalling.

Sweatpants, questionable grooming, and ratty T-shirts have no place in the classroom—especially not in a fashion classroom. I cracked down on the program's teachers. There were a lot of ruffled feathers. But they were feathers that needed ruffling. Imagine if one of these pajamas wearers said to a civilian, "I teach at the Parsons fashion program." One can say, "What we wear doesn't matter." But I always say, your clothes send a message about you. Without necessarily being conscious of it, you make snap judgments all the time based on appearances—and whether or not you think it's right, people are judging you, too. Period.

One day, one of these slobby, unwashed faculty members dismissed a student from her class for wearing a T-shirt with the F word on it. The student came to me and was visibly distraught. She said she'd never intended to upset anyone, and she couldn't stomach the notion she would have to leave class. She appealed to me, saying she believed that she was being unfairly judged. I listened and considered her appeal.

I brought the faculty member into my office.

"Do you remember our discussion about my expectations for the faculty's appearance?" I asked her. "Do you recall how I wanted you to make more of an effort to dress in a professional manner?"

"Yes," she said.

"Okay," I said. "Now let me make sure that I understand what you're saying. You're offended by the message the student is sending with her clothes. You don't like that her shirt says, literally, 'Fuck you.'"

"Yes."

"Well, to me," I said, "what *you* wear has 'fuck you' written all over it. It may not say that in words, but because of how sloppy you are, that is the message you are sending. This student is returning to your class. If you want to issue an edict on the first day of class that establishes rules of what you will and won't tolerate in your classroom, that's fine, and I will help you enforce those rules. No curse words? No hats? Whatever you say. Then if you want to throw a student out for failing to comply with your clearly stated rules, I will back you up a hundred percent. But you never told these students what they could and couldn't wear, and so you are not in a place to throw students out of your class on that basis. My advice is that you need to start dressing more professionally if you want your students to do the same."

When I was in a position to terminate people who were bad for the program, I took full advantage. There was no union at Parsons in those early and very formative years, so I had a lot of freedom. I could tell people they weren't coming back the following semester and I could bring in fresh blood. I got rid of a lot of people, which served to underscore my assessment that the fashion program I inherited was hemorrhaging.

There was one really problematic teacher. At registration the first September I was running the program, this guy sat with the program advisors and handpicked the students he wanted in his class: all men, and all cute. I was incredulous! And he'd been doing this for years and years. The sexual harassment of it all was so egregious. And no one had ever called him on it. "Why has this been tolerated?" I asked the administration. "It's the way things have always been," was their response. That spring I began to notice he was developing a growing arrogance about the annual senior fashion show.

My predecessor, Marie Essex, was ill with pancreatic cancer, and had stepped down as chair and taken a faculty position in the senior year. In deference to her years of service and experience—along with my newness—I had asked Marie to oversee the jury selection and the lineup of the show. But this ass was parading around like he was the king of the hill. "It's *my* show," I heard him say all too frequently. I took him aside. "It may be *Marie's* show. It may be *my* show," I said. "But it's definitely not *your* show."

I would have given just about anything to have fired him on the spot, but with only a month remaining in the semester, that seemed irresponsible. It would be easy to not renew his contract for the following year. But—and we all know people like this—he was one of those characters who, in spite of his obnoxious braggadocio and leering eye, had courted lots of support from a certain cadre of faculty. I thought it might be politically damaging to have the onus for his departure be on me.

How can I get this guy to quit? I wondered.

At the semester's end, I sent him a letter disinviting him from the fall registration session and stating that he would no longer be involved in the fashion show in any form. I added that I was aware he saw his students socially outside of class and I believed it to be considerably inappropriate. It was, I wrote, potential grounds for sexual harassment charges.

"I will ruin you!" he promised the next time I saw him.

He sent me a handwritten letter to that effect. It was like a medieval manuscript. He was a talented artist. It began, "I received your menacing missive."

And so he quit. I was ecstatic. I proudly hung his letter in my office bathroom. Once, while using the restroom, Diane von Furstenberg called out from behind the door, "What is a menacing missive?"

TEST DAY

There are some worrisome trends in the American education system. When Senator Kay Hagan (Democrat of North Carolina) spoke at a fund-raising event I held for her at my home, she said the North Carolina legislature wanted to get rid of all public education. Can you imagine? The University of North Carolina at Chapel Hill was the nation's first public university, and now you have North Carolina trying to completely privatize education and put the cost on to the parents? Things are bad enough without further separating out those with the money and means to give their children every advantage and those who are struggling just to get by. *This* is the investment we must make in our future!

Some states have talked about slashing their science curricula. Not only should there be more science, but we also need coding. Computer science is not going away. It's critical. Some places are moving in the opposite direction, and even banning the teaching of the theory of evolution. This is why I'm not necessarily in favor of leaving education up to the states. We all need the same knowledge, and I'd hate to think of a whole state full of children missing out on key parts of what they need to know just because of a few local politicians with specific agendas.

I've noticed that homeschooling seems to be on the rise. Given how poor our nation's test scores are these days, I am almost tempted to go in the other direction: let's make school residential. Don't let the kids go home! Have them stay 24/7. Keep studying! I'm joking, but when you see how we stack up to other countries, you start thinking extreme things.

Grading is an important aspect of our job as truth tellers. At colleges, there are often attempts at extortion around grading, such as: "We don't want him to lose his financial aid!" I have no patience for that stuff, at all. I believe testing is democratizing. Everything I read about the Common Core causes me to ask, "Why is everyone so hysterical?" Common Core charges the local municipality with coming up with structure and content. It's not a matter of the federal government handing down a syllabus and curriculum. Does anyone feel that education in this nation is adequate? I certainly don't. If we don't have some benchmarks for proficiency, how do we know how well we really are educating people? We've been operating with a blind trust that this is as good as it gets. Well, it's not good enough.

There's something to be said for rankings. As a competitive swimmer, the first time I came in third instead of fourth, fifth, or last was very motivating to me. Later, I came in second, and eventually one day I came in first. If you work hard, you can achieve practically anything.

When my sister started working at a school in rural Pennsylvania, she was director of testing, not just for the school, but for the region. (My sister, brother-in-law, and niece are all teachers. Teaching is in the blood.) When she began, between

3–5 percent of the kids from the region were eligible to take an untimed SAT. By the time she left twelve years later, it was more than 50 percent.

Special needs are very real and need to be accommodated. But if more than 50 percent of students fall into this category in a rural region, then what are we talking about? Similarly, I remember when ethnicity became a question on college applications. I was initially enthusiastic, because I thought it would help us ensure diversity, but ultimately I recall finding it hindered inclusivity, because more people checked "other" than anything else. And then we were right back to where we were before.

"My grandfather was my favorite teacher. He taught me how to draw three-dimensional ribbons and cubes. He was always so proud of me. My siblings and I used to fight to sit next to him on trips because he was so entertaining. As a teacher myself, my philosophy was to guide and encourage the direction the student was already going in. When you teach art, you have the power to critique someone's soul. So you need to be very careful."

—RITA, ART TEACHER, FLORIDA

As an examiner for the International Baccalaureate art and design credential, I traveled to I.B. schools around the nation to interview the candidates and see their portfolio of work in person. I loved those responsibilities, because I met some incredible—and inspiring—students and faculty. I was required to write an essay about each student. In addition, there were twenty-five to thirty questions for me about each I.B. candidate, and under each question would be choices, such as "always/sometimes/never. . . ." When I first began as an examiner, I found this process to be daunting (and extremely time-consuming), but I grew to love and respect it, because it so perfectly objectified my views and opinions.

Accordingly, I decided to formally share it with the fashion faculty. I said, "I want you to use this for your students as an assessment tool." Some were grateful for it. Others were annoyed, because they didn't like the idea of objective standards.

I hear so many parents wanting their children to opt out of state tests. Why? Students still have to follow the curriculum that leads up to that test. They just spend the test time apart from their testing classmates. And then their poor teachers have to go over all their work to come up with an assessment of whether or not they know the material rather than running a Scantron sheet. This pandering is bad.

I've heard that there's a new trend among overly zealous and simultaneously paranoid parents: seek an outside examiner, that is, someone who is not the teacher of the course. Talk about inappropriate and ridiculous.

Once a student of mine complained about the grade I'd given on an assignment. His parents took the work to an outside examiner for assessment. They returned to me and said, "Our outside examiner says this work is excellent and you don't know what you're talking about."

I bridled. "This examiner isn't looking at the work in the context of the class," I said. "My grade was based on a broad number of factors: what the assignment was, what the other students did, whether or not it was done by the deadline, how this work compares to the work presented for other assignments, and so on. This work was done in a context and received a grade in that context. Not to mention, I could bring in a slew of my own outside examiners who would say this work is terrible! But who cares? This is not up for discussion. I'm the teacher, and what I say in my class goes." I was really annoyed.

There was a *New York Times* op-ed called, "Save Us From the SAT."[2] That made me mad, too. Would you talk about the examinations one takes to become a doctor like that? There's licensing for doctors, for architects, for dentists, for interior designers, for real estate agents. Why wouldn't there be a similar process of evaluating credentials for the rest of us? Everyone else has tests that assess a base of knowledge. We need tests, too! Otherwise, how can we evaluate what's been learned? If you keep failing French I, you shouldn't go on to French II.

I like testing because it's democratic. I have a dear colleague whose daughter attended a fancy private school in New York City. This mother was insanely zealous about getting her into the best college possible. I don't even know how enthusiastic her daughter was about her mother's college goals for her, but that mother was going to get her daughter into the best school *come hell or high water.*

So, the girl had a class assignment due on the Duomo, the famous cathedral in Milan. Her mother, seeing this assignment as being an academic version of *The Amazing Race* and determined to give her every advantage, took her daughter on a weekend excursion to Milan. They took photos of the Duomo. They took a tour of the Duomo. They learned all there was to know about the Duomo. And in the process they ran into *another student from her class.*

Well, curses, this wouldn't do! The mother called everyone she knew—including Bill Clinton—to finagle a meeting with the cardinal of Milan. They got one. He didn't speak English, but they got that photo! And she trumped the other student and his parents. (Ladies and gentlemen, you can't make this stuff up.)

Well, I *thought* she'd trumped everyone. Then I met three well-spoken young men who were friends with this young lady. I learned that one had an assignment due on Angkor Wat, and so his parents flew him to Cambodia. Another had an assignment on the Hagia Sophia, and so his parents sent him to Turkey. The third, bless his deprived little heart, said that he didn't go anywhere.

When you think about how competitive college admission is, what do you do in the absence of test grades? Base it on whether there's a trip to Siem Reap, or whether Bill and Hillary call? It is extremely limiting when admissions aren't need-blind, because private colleges are so desperate for dough that they'll do anything to keep people. It turns the whole process into a joke.

"My favorite teacher was my [aptly named!] college professor Dr. Sun. She was kind, friendly, helpful, and cheerful. She was always willing to help anyone with anything and made the things taught in class easier to understand. She was always positive."

—MAI, RECENT COLLEGE GRADUATE, PENNSYLVANIA

I'm delighted to hear that the College Board is partnering with Khan Academy, the free online tutoring website, on which sharp teachers explain things like algebra or grammar. I like the whole premise. The concern I always had about test-prep companies was that they were teaching a test-taking strategy rather than actual knowledge and that their services were only accessible to those who could afford the fees.

One concern I have about the "new" SAT,[3] though: the revised SAT doesn't include obscure words.[4] I love those obscure words! They expand your horizons. Knowing them makes it easier to read great literature. Whenever I'm on a plane that hits turbulence, I open up the Mapp and Lucia books by E. F. Benson on my Kindle. They're from the twenties and thirties and they're very funny. I have them all. There are often out-of-fashion words in there. Every time I come across a word I don't know, I look it up on my Kindle. You can get a definition with just a tap!

And I will say that on a list of the 250 hardest old SAT vocabulary words, I was shocked to find only one I would consider truly obscure: "arrogate" (to claim something). In any case, I recognize that I am a lone voice howling in the wilderness on this one, and that language goes in and out of fashion in unpredictable ways.

I highly recommend *The Professor and the Mad Man*, a book about the writing of the Oxford English Dictionary. It's a totally compelling read. In it, we learn that the English-speaking world went *crazy* when the second edition came out. Their objection? The dictionary included contractions! As I keep repeating, everything has a context.

By way of an epilogue, I would like to add that out of those privileged, jet-setting high school students whom I mentioned earlier, the only one who was admitted to a top-tier school was the boy who, while his classmates were flying around meeting cardinals and touring Southeast Asian ruins, stayed home and kept his nose buried in a book.

"Elizabeth Drakeford, my seventh grade social studies teacher, was tough and demanding, and she quickly saw that I was performing far below my potential. I was smart, but I wasn't popular, so I performed on the nonchalant level of the popular kids in order to fit in. Mrs. Drakeford asked me to stay after class, and there she told me in no uncertain terms that she knew the game I was playing and she was not having it. She saw potential in me and refused to accept less than my best, in work and behavior. She was the first teacher to really believe in me, and I have never forgotten her or the lesson she taught me about self-respect.

"Later, Mrs. Connie Britt's music class, 'From Bach to Rock,' exposed me to an entirely new world. I came from humble beginnings, but because of Ms. Britt's passion for the finer things in life, now, thirty-four years later, I still love classical music, opera, ballet, art, and classic literature, all thanks to her."

—LISA, RETIRED GOVERNMENT EMPLOYEE, SOUTH CAROLINA

II

EMPATHY

E MPATHY IS THE CAPACITY to understand what other people are experiencing. It's essentially the golden rule: showing others respect and trying to put yourself in their shoes. In our interactions with others, we should always be asking ourselves: "How would I react if someone said or did this to me?" Most teachers of small children are excellent at empathy, and are constantly signaling their role as safe haven, like human light houses.

As mentors, we need to remember what it was like to be mentored. We need to think about all the great—and lousy and so-so—teachers we had and what it was like to be around them and to try to be on the side of right. The mentors on *Under the Gunn* had been in the same position, so they were able to bring real compassion to their designers.

In a critique, empathy is the stage at which you try to understand this particular designer—where they're coming from, what they hope to achieve, and what you may be able to do for them. Generally, empathy comes after truth telling and before pelting an individual with questions.

Here's a good example from outside the design world. My coauthor Ada's son, Oliver, who is seven, is taking chess. The other day, Ada told his teacher, Simon, that he was playing very well but often took a long time to checkmate his opponent (her), and that she felt a little like a mouse being toyed with by a cat that had nowhere to be.

Simon looked concerned. "It takes him a while to get the king?" Simon asked.

"Yes," Ada said.

"Do you have five minutes?" Simon asked.

"Sure."

"Oliver," Simon called, "please come over here. I want to show you something." And he set up the board in an endgame. There were temptations everywhere—pawns for the plucking, unguarded bishops. "What do you do?"

Oliver started to attack some of the unguarded pieces.

"No," Simon said. "Try again."

Oliver started going after pawns.

"No," Simon said. "Try again."

Oliver was confused. Why wouldn't he start grabbing pieces?

"What is the goal in chess?" Simon asked. "It's not to get as many pieces as you can. It's not to win on points. It's to get the king. Look at the board. How can you get my king? That should be the only question in your head."

Oliver stared at the board, and then his eyes lit up. In a couple of moves, he had won the game. Walking out of the room, he said, "Mom, I beat Simon!"

Of course, Simon was the one who had truly won. He'd come to understand something about his student's personality and style that could be a weakness for him. He immediately

took action to correct it. And in a few minutes, he improved his student's approach to the game forever, without even letting the child know he was learning something. There was no scolding or implication that he should have known already how to reach a checkmate. There was no shaming. A new skill was transmitted quietly and efficiently, because the lesson was personal and specific to that student's unique needs.

What's more, Simon accomplished that next-level teacher's trick of making Oliver feel as though he had come to this new skill entirely on his own. That is a mark of a teacher who is able to empathize with a child. He was able to deliver key information while allowing the student to preserve his or her integrity and security. And that's something for which we all need to strive.

"My high school art teacher, Jean Jarecke, was extremely supportive and encouraging. I've worked as an art consultant and teacher with all ages, from kindergarten to seniors. Giving students the ability to lose themselves in creating is rewarding for both of us. The students find themselves in the process. Also, exposing children who come from homes where art is nonexistent is amazing and a joy."
—JUDY, ARTIST, NEW YORK

PROJECT RUNWAY HOME VISITS

Empathy is about seeing where someone is coming from. That is literally what I do when I visit designers' homes for the home visits portion of each *Project Runway* finale. I meet their family and friends, see where they do their work, and get closer to the designer. It's one of the most fun and rewarding parts of the show for me. And on many occasions it has forced me to reevaluate a designer, for good or for ill.

For much of *Project Runway* Season 11, every time Patricia Michaels talked, my brain would bleed. She had this way of speaking nonstop, without taking a breath, for what felt like hours at a time. At the start of her home visit, on the Native American reservation where her family had lived for countless generations, I feared for my sanity, because I was a captive of Motor Mouth Michaels. There was no plumbing in the adobe, so we were walking across this snowy plain with buckets to get water from the stream. She kept talking on and on about her grandfathers and what seemed like every last cousin anyone had ever had. Finally, I said, in what I hoped was a polite attempt to get her to stop rambling, "Patricia, you need to write all this down! This is an incredible history. Preserve it."

She looked at me as though I had three heads. "I can't," she said. "Our culture doesn't permit it. We can't commit our history to written words. We can only transmit it by speaking it."

For me, it was like the lights came on. The fact that she was living by an oral tradition put everything about her that I'd found annoying into a new and quite beautiful context. She wasn't just talking to talk. She was talking to keep her culture alive. It was at that point that I relaxed with her. All my frustration dissipated. When you accept you can't change something, what else can you do but embrace it? I had an epiphany and, in the course of the visit, came to love and admire her.

During these home visits, I also learn so much more about the designers' preferred work methods and techniques. On the show, the workroom is stocked with standardized sewing machines and worktables, along with a common accessories wall. Going to the designers' homes, you see how they prefer things to be. Some workspaces are messy; some are neat. Some of the designers work in light-dappled manses; others work in dimly lit, mad-scientist caves. When you walk into their lairs, you see instantly what drives them and how they feel most comfortable.

Alexandria von Bromssen was very unemotional on the show. She came across as rather self-involved and uncaring. But then when I visited her home, I saw that she pours a tremendous amount of herself into a camp she runs for children. Showing off the children's work, she just lit up. She was so warm and nurturing with them. It was touching, and it made me much fonder of her.

On *Under the Gunn*, Oscar Garcia-Lopez's clothes often struck me as mysteriously older-ladyish. Here he was, a dynamic young man, and yet he was frequently making these old-fashioned garments. Well, then his mother and a family friend arrived for the show's finale. His mother came to visit, along with a sixty-something-year-old woman who was like a second mother to him. This was the woman he had referred to all season, and it became clear that she was his muse. Suddenly his aesthetic made so much more sense and it was really quite touching.

JURY DUTY

One of the great empathy inducers for me is jury duty. I'm proud to say that I've served on several juries, all of which were civil, but for one criminal trial. That was in 1994. The judge gave us a pep talk about the importance of the judicial system and the right to a trial by a jury of one's peers. I found him to be quite inspiring, but one of the women on the jury with me, a Park Avenue matron, piped up and said in a huffy lockjaw, "I'm sorry! But we are not his peers." The accused was a twenty-two-year-old homeless man who lived in a car and had held up a Chinese delivery person with the plastic knife in the bag of food. I gaped at the Park Avenue matron. I'm not saying such behavior is acceptable, but whenever I see someone in such dire straits, my first reaction is not "That could never be me!" but rather: "There but for the grace of God go we all."

Anyway, jury duty makes you realize a lot about humanity. This particular trial was right after the O. J. Simpson circus, so there were people on the jury who thought the accused was the victim of a police conspiracy, which made it hard for us to reach a verdict. The discussions were brutal, and every day brought more delays until we ended up sequestered for two nights. We were taken to the Staten Island Inn in a bus with bars on the windows. It was my first time going to Staten Island and I must say that the view of Manhattan from the Verrazano-Narrows Bridge is spectacular, even looking at it through bars.

One woman on the jury with me was named Mrs. Porter, although she was constantly telling everyone, "It's pronounced Por-TAY." She kept stealing the silverware each morning at breakfast and her purse became heavier and noisier with each day. I was having tea at the inn that second morning and Mrs. Por-Tay asked me to hand her the silver teapot. I said, "There's no water left." She said, "I don't want the water. I want the teapot."

In addition to the cutlery klepto, there were three conspiracy theorists on the jury who were never going to let the defendant be found guilty. My earlier pride in the carrying out of civic duties was quickly eroding into complacency and depression. Not to mention the fact that I had been wearing the same clothes—and underwear!—for three days.

The afternoon of our last day of deliberations, the forewoman of the jury said to me, "Tim, you've been uncharacteristically quiet today."

"That," I said, "is because I've been looking around this room trying to figure out ways to kill myself."

"Oh, Tim," she said with a laugh, "we'd never let you do that!"

"Don't think," I responded, "that my plan doesn't include killing all of you first."

Luckily, that day we declared we were a hung jury and we were allowed to finally go home.

"Rose Scozzafava (we all called her 'Scozz'), was my junior high school chorus teacher in Rockville, MD. Scozz made being in the chorus cool, and thus attracted football players, nerds, cheerleaders, lovers of music, good students, and not so good ones. We were a diverse team! She insisted we all learn to read music. We learned choral compositions generally considered to be too difficult for kids our age. Along with our music, we learned discipline. Everyone had to memorize the music—no paper used in performances. We wore white shirts and black pants or skirts, and stood ramrod straight. (God forbid if your nose itched, because you knew you couldn't raise your arm to scratch.) Our chorus won statewide awards. We all loved Scozz and loved singing for her. Many of us went on to obtain music degrees (myself included)."

—LAUREL, RETIRED CORPORATE EXECUTIVE, ARIZONA

THE SUPERMARKET

I spend a good deal of time at the Food Emporium near my apartment on the Upper West Side. (I buy a lot of paper towels. When I leave this planet, sell off all your stock in paper, because the industry will tumble without me there to support it.) At the supermarket, I find endless examples of questionable behavior. Why, for example, do the people in front of me in line always seem shocked when they get to the cash register and have to get out their wallets? Why no preparation? All that time waiting in line, and it never once seemed like a good time to get ready?

When I go to the grocery store, I often chat with the manager or the two assistant managers. I'll ask them what's fresh and they'll help me figure out what to make for dinner. The other day I was waiting in line and I saw a woman storm back in and yell at the grocery bagger. She dumped her grocery bags back on the counter and said, "Why would you do this?"

"What did I do?" the bagger asked.

"Why would you put two bottles of soda in the same bag?" the customer yelled. "I want this bottle moved!"

Why don't you remove it yourself? I thought. But the bagger simply apologized and rebagged the soda.

When I got to the front, I said to the bagger, "I thought you handled that very well. I don't know that I would have been as calm in the face of such rudeness. She should have shown more respect to you and the work you do all day." I am endlessly fascinated by the egregious behavior faced by baggers and checkout people, and how calmly they greet it. They are saints among us.

Seriously, how horrible is it when people abuse those who are doing things for them? I always blanch when I see someone cold-shoulder a waiter. If you don't interact with waitstaff, how will you get served? We each have a job to do, and we should respect people who are doing their jobs.

Well, in anticipation of Hurricane Sandy, the Food Emporium was wiped out of nearly everything on the shelves. By Wednesday, two days after the storm hit, things were looking good. By Thursday, everything was more or less back to normal. But on Saturday, I was in the cheese aisle and saw a woman berating the manager. "I cannot believe you don't have any mascarpone cheese!" she was yelling.

Here we were, so fortunate to be in the upper half of Manhattan with water and electricity and *food*, whereas the lower half of the city was largely evacuated. Now, I almost never butt in, but in this case I couldn't help saying something. I hate to see someone bullied, and the store manager looked like he was about to cry.

"Excuse me," I said to the woman. "May I suggest that this is a minor and temporary inconvenience? Many people lost everything this week. Surely we can soldier on without mascarpone cheese for another day or two, or however long it takes?"

She just stared at me, looking rather horrified. I looked back at her in horror, too. There were people whose homes were destroyed! How could she be getting so worked up about cheese? Not to mention, for what she was making, ricotta or cream cheese would have been a perfectly acceptable substitute. And the store had both.

Another thing I hate is when people put their cart in line and then continue to shop. I just witnessed it, again, yesterday. And frankly, if I'm behind the cart and the person's not back, I simply go ahead. Using placeholders in stores? Please. We're grown-ups.

Really, I find gratuitous displays of privilege or entitlement troubling. I remember when a famous college was recruiting a friend of mine to be on its board. My friend was honored and eager to serve. But then she ran into the president of the college at an airport. When she looked past this man and out the window, she saw a jet that had the school's name emblazoned on it. Her eyes turned back to the president, whom she fixed with a stare. "You have a private plane? I'm no longer interested in being on your board or giving you money. Good day." And she walked away, ignoring his protests. Hear, hear.

"My third grade teacher was so patient with me that, thanks to her, I really love to read and teach kids. Miss Carmelita marked my life with love and patience. She really made a difference in my life. Teaching: It's the privilege only for those who have a generous heart. *Dar clases es un privilegio solo para aquel de corazon generoso!*"
—WILLY, TEACHER, MEXICO

SHOPPING AT MOOD

Anyone who has watched *Project Runway* knows that the show is inextricable from a prime fabric and notions resource, Mood. I love going shopping at Mood. And I've found that most of the designers I bring there are professional and well organized. They go down the aisles they need to go down, pull a few bolts, have the material cut, and head to the cash registers. But some designers are not like this. They meander. They second-guess. They have more things cut than they can use. In short, they make life very difficult for those around them.

In all areas of life, high-maintenance people make me crazy, and I avoid them whenever I can. In my world, the squeaky wheel does *not* get the grease. People who give in to that harassment have only themselves to blame. It's harder in the short term, but so much easier in the long term. Whenever someone would try to push my buttons, Marsha, my deft assistant chair at Parsons, would give me an *uh-oh* face, because she knew what was coming. Yes, that meeting would be over in a nanosecond. (By the way, never have student meetings alone.

You need the corroboration of a peer. I'm more than happy to have faculty meetings alone, unless I think there will be a contentious issue, in which case I have a peer sit in there, too. Protect yourself from potentially incendiary situations.)

Natalia Fedner was an example of a high-maintenance individual, and that made her a controversial figure on *Under the Gunn* Season 1. When she was voted off for a poorly constructed pink dress midway through the show, I thought the decision was fair. I also thought it had been a long time coming.

When I saw she'd been cast, I expected a rocky road. She'd been a student at Parsons when I was there. I found her to be extremely motivated and talented. I never had any issues with her finishing work, ever. But then, it wasn't *Project Runway*. However, as chair of the department, I'd heard all her *woe is me* stories. I'd been inclined to believe that she was truly being victimized by faculty members and oppressed. She later told me she was sorry she'd gone to Parsons in the old days, before I got rid of the faculty who gave her so much grief.

And yet, I've come to think that wouldn't have made a difference. She seems to navigate the world as a victim. When she broke down on the runway in Week 1, I thought, *We need to get her out of here*. In my book, when you see that dramatic a reaction and presentation, you have to figure it's not aberrant. That's who that person is. And you're going to get more of it. And we did get more of it. She made bad judgments again and again. She didn't properly calibrate her time. She didn't understand her model's measurements in spite of the fitting. And she was seldom, if ever, ready to go to the runway when I would call time.

But what drove me—and everyone else—to despair was that she was so dramatic, it made life difficult for everyone. While at Mood, I would call time and her fabric would still be uncut. Her inability to make decisions would lengthen our trip by twenty to forty minutes every time, the consequence being less time in the workroom. Half an hour may not sound like much, but when you only have one day for a challenge, it feels like a lifetime, and it really adds up in the course of a month. Understandably, this angered the designers and mentors. She constantly sought affirmation for her work from the other designers, too, thereby distracting them and taking up more of their time. Finally, she was incapable of calibrating her design and execution ambitions to our time frame. It was frustrating and soul sucking for all.

And so, when she went home, I thought, *phew!* But then on Twitter and Facebook there was an outcry of, "Poor Natalia!" I was accused of bullying her, and of siding against her with other designers who were being mean. Well, I read all those angry comments in response to the perception that Natalia was bullied on the show. To that I say, "Balderdash!"

Does anyone think I would tolerate such a thing? I have a great deal of affection and respect for Natalia and have known her for fourteen years. I can attest to her high level of talent and aptitude. Everyone—designers, mentors, me—only wanted Natalia to succeed. And we only wish her the greatest success.

But as a department chair, and even earlier as associate dean of Parsons, I learned the hard way that there are always *at least* two sides to every story. Usually more. I say, "I learned the hard way," because I was burned with a good deal of frequency when I would act upon one side of a story without first engaging in investigation and research. I learned to always probe and query. It was never 100 percent how it was portrayed by the first person to tell me the story. All the stories I heard were about 60 percent true. After doing the due diligence, talking to people separately, I would then bring them into the same room together to talk about it. In Natalia's case, I determined that the other designers were justifiably annoyed with her and that their irritation was legitimate and quite moderate given the extent of the irritant.

Sensitive people will often talk about how other people are "triggering" them. Well, someone told me recently that my hairline is receding and I'm getting a bald spot. I didn't mind. It's true! It's a matter of fact rather than their being mean. Being mean, in my view, is teasing someone in a manner calculated to cause shame, or acting hateful because of something they can't change. But stating a fact like "Natalia, your inability to make decisions is causing a problem for us," is not mean. That's just truth telling.

And an epilogue: two days after losing my temper with Natalia at Mood, I returned to the store to speak to the Mood sales associate who had been helping her. I wanted to apologize for losing my temper, and to also say I was sorry that Natalia had given her such a hard time. The sales associate wasn't there. "She went home with a migraine right after you left," her colleague told me, "and we haven't seen her since."

"Miss Broverman, my ninth-grade English teacher, was a formidable older lady who had a reputation for giving no quarter. She rarely smiled, she was a stickler for enunciation, and all students were Mister or Miss. She scared the pudding out of me, but I learned so much about English literature and Shakespeare that year. Miss Broverman always told us what she expected from us (a LOT), always gave us the tools we needed to achieve those goals, and never made anyone feel like a failure. She expected us to work, learn, earn our grades, and expand our horizons. Fairness ruled, respect was earned, and she never forgot a student. Years and years after I had graduated and moved to a different state, my mom told me that whenever she would run into Miss Broverman when she was out and about, Miss Broverman would ask, 'And how is Laurie doing?'"

—LAURIE, RETIRED SOCIAL WORKER, TEXAS

CHURCH

I attended Sunday School for years, but I don't remember anything about it. I do remember our crazy Episcopal priest. I hated going to church largely because of him. He would go into these silent prayers that would last forever. Often during these prayers he would fall asleep, leaving us all shifting anxiously in our pews. One Sunday, as he slept, two parishioners went up to the pulpit and took him away, and he never came back. I confess to you that I gloated. I'd always told my parents that he was peculiar.

Bible stories are very profound. Having moral lessons rooted in stories makes them so much more powerful. You can tell a child all day long to be generous, but if you don't show him or her why, or how, then what use is it? If you tell a child the story of the widow's penny, the Bible story in which a poor widow gives a cent to the treasury even as rich men are putting in great sums and Jesus says that she has given more than anyone, it teaches that child about the outsize power of small generous actions. Using a story to convey that moral contextualizes the lesson.

I'm not religious these days, but I'm close to many people who are. My niece teaches at a Catholic boarding school, and she has come to deeply appreciate that religion. For her, it's about the ceremony. She was confirmed in the Episcopal church, and now she's talking about becoming confirmed as a Catholic.

When I was a child, we attended St. Albans, the church behind the National Cathedral. I hated going to church so much that when my father stopped at a stop sign, I would jump out of the car and run home. I found church an excruciating waste of valuable time that could be better spent reading or playing with Legos.

The other day I was wondering why we drove rather than walked, as it wasn't far from our house. But then I realized: my father would drop us off and then drive around "looking for a parking space." He often arrived halfway through the service or later. I believe he cherished that time alone.

My grandmother was the primary churchgoer in the family. Her church was St. John's Church, across from the White House. They wouldn't marry my sister there because she wasn't a regular member, like our grandmother. Well, my grandmother found that extremely petty. She called the bishop of Washington and asked if he would marry her granddaughter at our home, and he said yes, of course. Well, my grandmother never went back to St. John's. She was dead a year later, but still.

SPEAKING ENGAGEMENTS

At a recent fund-raising dinner I attended, every single speaker but one read their speeches without once looking out at the audience. I was shocked. If you don't make eye contact, you don't engage with the audience, and you are apt to lose them in the first fifteen seconds. When you're speaking to a group, whether you're teaching or giving a speech, you should at least look at them and say hi. That way they know you're in the room and you're not just a talking head.

Once I was told I had to read prepared remarks, and I did it, but I apologized profusely first. "I'm so sorry to read from these cards," I said, "but I was just given them and I don't want to ramble and disappoint our host." At another event, I had to present with someone else, and in that case, too, I understood why I was handed cards right before going out. "This is like twin pianos, for which both players should have sheet music," I told my co-presenter when she apologized for the cards. "It would be irresponsible for either of us to be up here without the remarks."

I enjoy public speaking now, but I wasn't always so comfortable giving presentations. My first year in admissions at

Parsons, I had to go on the road to present the school to various groups of potential applicants. This was primarily in high schools. I had been teaching for five years, so I believed that I understood how best to present and how to read an audience. I was three weeks into what they call roadwork. It was 1983, before PowerPoint, and so I had a tray of slides that I traveled with. My boss, Kit Chase, came out to spend the day with me to give me feedback. I was so proud of my presentation. I thought I was presenting good and very relevant information about the way the school fostered the creative process.

I was enamored of Kit, who is lovely and sweet and very thoughtful, but after she sat through my first presentation, she said, "I'm sorry, but that may have been the worst presentation I've ever seen in my life. Usually I would wait until the end of the day to offer a critique, but that was so terrible that we have to fix it now." And there were a mere forty-five minutes before the next presentation.

During this awful presentation, I had talked about the stages of development from a drawing to a prototype, and she said that was exactly the wrong thing to talk about. She took my carefully arranged eighty slides and dumped the tray containing them upside down on the dashboard of our rental car. I felt devastated and humiliated, but what is one to do other than stiff-upper-lip-it and carry on.

"Talk about careers," she said, shuffling my slides. "Talk about outcomes after Parsons. Divide it up by disciplines." She was right. I'd been living in my own fools' paradise. It was startling to me.

She did the next presentation to show me. And I did the third one and did it more like her version—anything to please her. Eventually I found my own way of doing it that I was com-

fortable with. It's extremely valuable to be evaluated by someone with experience and success in your field. The students
and teachers in the classes I visited had never met me before.
To them my presentations weren't bad. They just didn't offer
information that was valuable for them. Because of my own
background, I was so used to fine arts and the creative process
that I didn't think of careers. In fine arts, it's all about your soul
and your passion, right? That's what I thought. But Kit made
me see that for prospective students there's a lot more to it. I'm
forever grateful to her.

"Ms. Miller, my second-grade teacher, always went above
and beyond to not only listen, but to excite and engage the
kids. She shared her love of rock collecting with me and I
(for a while) was very into rocks. She retired after her year
teaching me, and consented to being my pen pal. I have no
idea what I wrote to her, but getting a real letter in the mail
made me feel so grown up. It was a little thing to her, but
it meant the world to me and I'll never forget her. Now that
I'm a knitting teacher, I focus on teaching the 'why,' not just
the 'how.'"

—PATTY, KNITTING TEACHER AND DESIGNER, NEW YORK

READING ONLINE COMMENTS

I work hard to be kind to everyone, and yet I still sometimes find myself hurting people's feelings. I do dozens of interviews a month sometimes. In one of these in February 2014, for the *Huffington Post*, the lovely reporter asked me about something in my last book about Gaultier's use of a transgender model for women's clothes and, even more pointed, my view of transgender models walking the runways at New York Fashion Week.

I repeated what I had said in the book: that I thought diversity was wonderful but I didn't think in the case of the high-fashion world that the designers were doing this to be more inclusive. Both there and in the case of the more real-world and, therefore, accessible clothes shown at New York Fashion Week, I saw it as designers and their casting agents trying to find models with yet another unattainable—by most women—body.

First we had eating disorders in proliferation all over the runways; then we had models who had undergone limb-lengthening surgery (I kid you not); and now we have women without hips. Of those three examples, the latter is the least attainable of all. Women have hips—period. When the average size in America is a 14, why is it that models are always a 0? And now even that is apparently too big, so that designers are looking to male skeletons that by design have no hips at all! Maybe I was just being cynical, but in my eyes, the fervor wasn't about getting these transgender men-to-women into the public eye to help promote them. It was, "Hallelujah! Women with no hips! Our new muse!"

The quote that ran in the *Huffington Post*[1] was this: "It underscores all of those body issues that we know women have. It's the world telling us that there's something wrong with us and that we'd look better in our clothes and the world would think us more beautiful if we looked like this. I think it's horrible."

And it was rendered on a slew of other blogs as variations on this: "Tim Gunn Thinks Trans Models are Horrible." As if! I would like to say here and now that I think it is wonderful that there are transgender models, and I am deeply sorry if anyone felt that I was saying otherwise. Diversity is always a good thing, and we must all follow our passions. Star trans model Andrej (now Andreja) Pejic is beautiful, and it's no wonder designers want to use her. My only question—and I meant it only as a question, not as a policy position—is whether it was an example of the fashion industry's ongoing opposition to womanly hips.

I was not prepared for the reaction. Calls and emails flooded in calling me all sorts of names. I was accused of "bone structure essentialism," transphobia, and ignorance.[2] A representative with the Human Rights Campaign, a gay-rights group to which I have donated countless hours and dollars for more than a decade, contacted me and demanded an apology. I asked if I could speak with my colleague there on the phone. I was told that until I issued a formal apology for my remarks, he would not even take my call.

How is that conducive to my fully understanding the source of the fury, and to my explaining what I was awkwardly trying to say? That hurt more than anything. I was shocked that one line in an interview, in which I thought I was merely asking a question about the motivation behind a trend, could undo my many years of hard work on behalf of all members of the LGBTQ community. Why wouldn't this man take the initiative, call me, and say, "Tim, you've been such a supporter of gay rights over the years. Please help me understand what you said in this interview, because I find it concerning?" I would respect that approach so much more than what he did, which was tantamount to shutting me out completely and issuing the statement, "J'accuse!"

The HRC wasn't alone. Another organization I have supported in various ways over the years, the Gay & Lesbian Alliance Against Defamation (GLAAD), also went on the offensive. I was notified that because of my *Huffington Post* comments, GLAAD may make *Project Runway* ineligible to win the award for which we'd been nominated.

Amid the furor, Pejic tweeted, "Wow Tim Gunn is at it again! Attacking the little diversity there is in fashion in support of diversity??? And for ur info I happen to have a female type pelvis :)."[3]

To her point: what I was trying clumsily to say was that while I fully support transgender models and feel they should be on all runways, I wonder if adding gorgeous, ultraskinny male-to-female transgender models to the roster of gorgeous, ultraskinny cisgender female models promotes body-type diversity. To me it looked like less diversity: just ever-skinnier girls.

But I am sorry she felt disrespected in any way. I heard and respected her comment. I hated that I caused Pejic or anyone else any grief. I didn't sleep for days. I was racked with guilt that I might have hurt anyone.

I have since been made aware that transgender people do in fact come in all shapes and sizes, and that some transgender women do have hips. (As a fact-checking note, though: I've been in the same room with Pejic, and she is magnificently beautiful and regal and deserves all the success and praise in the world, but on behalf of the average-size women of America: the svelte Ms. Pejic has all the voluptuous, womanly curves of a tongue depressor.)

In any case, I'm sorry for suggesting that all transgender bodies look the same, or giving anyone the impression that I would tolerate the exclusion of transgender women from any realm whatsoever. As I hope my decades of activism on this front prove, I have no tolerance for bullying of any kind, and I believe very strongly in the mainstream acceptance of all gay, lesbian, transgender, bisexual, and questioning people.

I also hope we can discuss these things openly. Not long after the HRC, GLAAD, and what felt like the whole Internet took me to task, I saw RuPaul criticized for using the word "tranny" on *RuPaul's Drag Race*. I was very happy to see the transgender performer Our Lady J's essay defending Ru.[4] She said that over-policing language "threatens the core of our creative abundance."

When a CEO was pushed out of his job for supporting Proposition 8 (a proposal to ban gay marriage that I went to great lengths to help defeat), Andrew Sullivan wrote: "If we are about intimidating the free speech of others, we are no better than the anti-gay bullies who came before us."[5] I agree with him. As an educator, I hope that we one day get to a point where we can hash out these issues in public and maybe make mistakes. Political correctness comes from a well-meaning place, but it can be destructive to the educational process of searching for answers in a nonjudgmental space, and of trial and error. When I hear people say things I might consider ignorant, I try very hard to see it as an opportunity to educate, not to shame.

"My English teacher Jon Ummel, who taught at Mountlake Terrace High School in Washington State, wasn't your typical teacher. He knew how to get down to the level of a high schooler and get them to listen. We once had a writing assignment about heroes. To jump-start our thinking process, we watched *The Empire Strikes Back*, and Mr. Ummel shared with us his great Darth Vader impression. He was always kind. He never put anyone down for any idea. He never raised his voice. He made the writing assignments fun—which is a great trick for getting people to learn something."

— TINA, EXECUTIVE ASSISTANT, WASHINGTON

NAVIGATING ACADEMIC POLITICS

Parsons has always thought of itself as being a progressive academic institution. When it was founded in 1896 as The Chase School (after the American painter William Merritt Chase), it caused quite a stir. The reason? Men and women coexisted in life-drawing classes. Scandalous! Ten years later, in 1906, Frank Alvah Parsons, for whom the school would later be renamed, joined the faculty and created the first design programs in the nation—fashion, interior architecture, and advertising art (graphic design).

This was a new threshold for design in America, but Parsons also saw a nation that was anemic when it came to historic and societal precedents for these emerging disciplines. Accordingly, Parsons looked to Europe and opened study centers in London, Paris, and Florence. Beginning in 1920, a year of study abroad was required of every student who wished to receive a diploma. This progressive institution was now international.

One of my jobs as associate dean at Parsons was to be the liaison to our programs abroad—Paris and the Dominican

Republic, at the time of my appointment—and to work with the development of new programs—Kanazawa, Japan; Seoul, South Korea; and Kuala Lumpur, Malaysia. In Malaysia, our work was with the government. The prime minister's daughter was a Parsons grad and he was enthralled with both the quality of her education and the pronounced difference that he perceived in corresponding design colleges in his nation. I was sent to Kuala Lumpur for two weeks, ostensibly, but that two weeks turned into four months.

I learned so much during my time there. I had never even visited a Muslim nation, let alone lived in one. There were many cultural and societal challenges for me, and in spite of having researched the do's and don'ts, I made many a gaffe. My first happened the day after I arrived. I was invited to dinner and I accepted. Gaffe! My acceptance was an egregious act of rudeness; one must be asked three times before accepting. That had never come up in my research. Handshaking had—*don't*. When one greets someone, a small bow from the waist is the acknowledgment.

And then there was something that I found to be deeply troubling, because it represented racism, plain and simple. There are three distinct classifications of people in Malaysia: Indian Malays, Chinese Malays, and Bumiputeras. The latter group are the "native" Malays and the name roughly translates to "sons of the soil." This is a greatly favored population and at least 51 percent of the employees of any organization must be Bumiputeras. Furthermore, like civil servants elsewhere, it can be close to impossible to fire a Bumiputera.

Sad to say, many therefore get by doing less. The Chinese Malays are considered to be the banking and finance people. And the Indian Malays are perceived to be working-class and laborers. Do you see a corollary? Skin color: the darker your skin, the further down you are in the food chain. I was horrified, but I had to stomach it. Tim Gunn certainly wasn't going to single-handedly alter this culture.

Especially not after this cultural aberration slapped me directly in the face, caused unintentional pain to another, embarrassed a third party, and made me look like an ignorant, ugly American. What happened, you ask? I was interviewing scores of individuals for the position of dean of the college, the very top administrative position. I found someone who took my breath away, because she possessed every characteristic that I believed would be required to lead this new enterprise. She was an experienced teacher and administrator, had created innovative academic programming in Australia, and knew how to think outside of the proverbial box. I loved her.

The whipped cream on top was the fact that this was one of the most stunning and elegant women I had ever encountered. This top appointment was the only one for which I had to seek the approval of the prime minister. I made an appointment with him to discuss the candidate, and she and I arrived at his grand office together. His assistant greeted us and I introduced him to her.

"And when," he asked, "is the candidate for the dean's position arriving?"

"This is the candidate," I responded.

Well, this guy can never play poker; the look that he gave her and me said it all.

"Mr. Gunn, may I see you in my office?"

I followed. To make a long story a little bit shorter, he said that it was an outrage and an insult to have brought an Indian

Malay and—he wasn't finished—a *woman* to meet with the prime minister. He declared that neither would be acceptable to "Sir."

So now it's racism and misogyny, too? I thought. I could take this beating, but now I had to tell the dean candidate that she had been rejected on such shallow grounds. Not to mention: I didn't have a second favorite to bring before the prime minister. There was no one else even close in the running. In the end, we wound up hiring an incredibly dynamic woman from New York—since she was not a native, her gender did not pose the same problem for Sir.

"Mrs. Eagan, my high school literature teacher, was happy with her life, and that transferred into the classroom. She liked everyone and had no favorites. She had great reading lists, and the discussions were lively and fun and gave me a lifelong love of reading."
—LINDA, RETIRED, IOWA

On the topic of recruiting faculty in Malaysia: I heard more horror stories. I found out that, culturally, it was not good for anyone to stand out; that is, don't upstage anyone, don't shout out when you know the answer and no one else does, don't distinguish yourself above others. Malaysian faculty taught to the lowest common denominator, and they were very matter-of-fact about it. Competition was looked upon as a Western anomaly and it must be prevented from entering the culture. I thought, *What are we going to do? How can this school happen unless we change this culture?*

I explained that the reason this design college was being launched was to bring an American flavor of education to Malaysia. At this school, competition will be and must be celebrated. The prospective students were baffled, and so were many of the prospective faculty members. I was speaking a foreign language to them, and they had no corresponding words in their own vocabulary that allowed them to process what I was saying. In my experience, a competitive environment is a catalyst for students to do a higher level of work. Otherwise, there's no incentive or motivation to push yourself.

Just one more story about this project and I promise we will move on: the academic facility. I was working out of an office in a government building. This was merely a temporary situation until the once beautiful but now decrepit national historic landmark building was remodeled. I drove past that building every day to and from my hotel and office. I kept inquiring about its status, because there was no evident progress.

One day our small administration had an audience with "Sir" and his senior advisors. (I was in regular communication about the status of the project with most of those advisors.) During this meeting, the prime minister stated that invitations were being sent out for a ribbon cutting at the college two weeks from that very day.

What? I'm looking around the room and no one is flinching; there's not a single indication of unease. People are talking enthusiastically about guest lists; press, including television; the *datuks* and *datins* (think princes and princesses). I couldn't stand it any longer. There was a lull, so I seized it.

"Sir," I said, "have you seen the college site recently? I'm very concerned that two weeks will not be adequate to prepare the facility for a ceremony."

Well, every attendee at the meeting, with the exception of Sir, gave me a *die-scum-die* look.

"Why do you say that, Mr. Gunn?" Sir asked.

"I think you should see it, Sir, and make the decision," I said.

You want to know what his response was? "I'll send my wife."

So, I met Mrs. Sir at the historic site that was to be our campus. I wish I had taken photographs or videotaped that entire session. She was stunned.

Nothing, but nothing, had been done to the building. It would have to be improved to even qualify as a slum. Well, the next day architects and workers arrived! But when I returned to New York after my four-month stint there, the building still wasn't ready for a ribbon cutting! Things move slowly in Malaysia . . .

Frankly, I found the academic politics worrisome in all of our programs abroad. For one of the schools, we partnered with the city of Kanazawa Chamber of Commerce, on the Sea of Japan. One of the leaders of the project was a dynamic woman out of Tokyo named Reiko. She ran a public relations firm and had a very high profile. She was the dealmaker between the Chamber and Parsons. She remained intimately involved throughout the entire development of the college and I worked very closely with her.

On the opening day of the school, I was sitting in the library talking to faculty members. The elevator doors open into the library. I see Reiko. She looks distraught. I get up to go toward her to congratulate her on the opening, and she shrieks,

"Not you! My assassin!" I was baffled. Finally, the Parsons dean, my boss, appeared. When I asked what happened, he said, "Oh, I fired her because of the poor enrollment, and I blamed the decision on you."

That's when I threw away all my bow ties, because the dean wore them.

This man also possessed one of my least favorite academic habits: wanting other people to call him "doctor," even though he just has a doctorate of fine arts. I have one, too! The Corcoran gave me an honorary doctorate several years ago, and I cherish the honor. But until I can perform heart surgery, you will never hear me introduce myself as Doctor Gunn.

My philosophy is: if you can't suture a wound, don't call yourself a doctor. Some people have two PhD's. Do we call them Doctor Doctor? I guess I can understand it in an academic field, but not in the field of practice, like fine art. I find it so pretentious. I imagine an announcement made over a PA: "Is there a doctor of fine arts in the house? We need to analyze this painting STAT!"

On an early trip to Korea, I got my index finger stuck in the seat on Northwest Airlines (that's how long ago it was). It sounds impossible and idiotic, but it's true. There was blood everywhere. I almost severed it. Dr. Dean, whom I was sitting next to, was asleep through the whole thing, even as a real doctor—an M.D.—from elsewhere on the plane came by and bandaged me up.

"I've been thinking," my seatmate said dreamily when he awoke. "When we land, whenever you use my name, I'd like it to be with my title: Doctor."

"Sure," I said. "Providing you can you fix *this*, Dr. Olton." I held my heavily bandaged hand up to him.

"Ms. Allison, my high school English teacher at a rather uptight, very traditional, all-girls Catholic high school, appeared very prim and proper on the outside, but she had an adventurous spirit. The other girls came from families of 'breeding,' and loved the traditions, pomp, and pageantry of it all. I did not. Questioning authority and traditions was not the way to make friends at that school. Ms. Allison encouraged me to challenge the status quo. She told me I was smart and should never let anyone tell me how to think, and that I should never be ashamed or afraid to swim against the current. She allowed me to break rank with the standard curriculum and write my term papers on authors who spoke to my teen angst. Many of the other students shunned her because she was weird. I adored her because not only did she march to her own drummer, she encouraged me to make my own drum and beat it loudly."

—TERI, TEXTILE PRINTER, NORTH CAROLINA

Years later, I was delighted when that man went on to become president of what was then called the American Symphony Orchestra League: ASOL. Pronounce it like a word, not an acronym, and you have the perfect distillation of my opinion of him.

Annoying administrators can make your life as a teacher genuinely miserable. One stands out in my mind. During my time at the Corcoran School of Art (now College of Art) in Washington, D.C., she actually said out loud: "I'm feeling very dean-y today!" These people are comic relief, except when they are making your life a living hell.

She was especially tone-deaf when it came to those less fortunate than she was. She was giving a speech once in the school's large and classically adorned auditorium—and let me tell you that she had a memorable presence, sort of a Julia Child in stature and voice, but absent the charm. She spoke forever, leading off with the immortal line: "This auditorium reminds me of the salon in my large, hospitable household." We in the faculty looked at one another and rolled our eyes so far back in our heads that we almost went blind.

When I was teaching at the Corcoran, we were going through the reaccreditation process. This was for the Middle States Association of Colleges and Schools (MSACS). The commissioner, a dynamic woman out of Philadelphia named Minna Weinstein, was overseeing the review. She told us the goals in broad strokes: "It's all about who you are as an institution, what your goals are, and how well you are achieving them."

I didn't mean to be sarcastic, but I said, "So, if our goal is to be the worst art and design program in the nation, and we are, do we get accredited?"

A wonderful sport, she laughed and said with a smile, "Well, we would challenge that goal."

Anyway, we had to have an executive from the D.C. school system be a part of the process. This lovely woman showed up. I greeted her and introduced her to the acting dean: "This is Dr. Smith from the D.C. school system, here for the accreditation process."

The administrator just stared at her, blankly, making not a single utterance. It was rather like that cliff-hanging moment in Agatha Christie's *The Mirror Crack'd*.

I tried to ignore how rude she was, and quickly escorted Dr. Smith back to the reception area. Then I returned to the administrator's office and said, "You seem disturbed by this D.C. executive. Is something wrong?"

"She's black!"

"Yes?" I said.

Again: "This doctor. She's black!"

There was a pause while I gaped at the dean.

"I don't know how to respond to this," I finally said. "What's the issue?"

"My God!" she said. "If they're not picking up your garbage, they're doctors!"

I glared at her and walked out. It was horrifying.

Another time, I arrived with a colleague at this woman's home for a college-wide event.

"You're late!" she said to my companion, who was black. "And please go around to the service entrance."

I was aghast and stared daggers at her. "May I please introduce you to the estimable Ted Sherron, president of the Cleveland Institute of Art?"

"Oh!" she said. "Well, come in."

"I'd rather not, actually," he said, justifiably, and turned around and left.

She and I disagreed often, including once during an open house for prospective students. In one of the studios, a student had left a project that she took objection to: a six-foot papier-mâché penis, painted in flesh tones. She said that there should be a "no-genitalia" rule for the students' work.

"So," I said, "you'd be with the popes, whacking off the genitalia of Michelangelo's sculpture."

She blushed, and seemed flattered to be compared to the popes.

It's not a compliment, you loon! I thought.

"That's censorship," I said. "This work exists, and it deserves to exist."

"It shouldn't be allowed to exist!" she said.

The compromise was that we would hide it from the tour, and then replace it before the student returned. And that is how we wound up running away from the touring families through the school, holding either end of a giant phallus—she commandeering the front and me the back—until we found a place to hide it. The penis ended up taking a holiday in the boiler room.

"Jack Taylor, my sixth grade teacher, made each and every one of us feel loved. He did not teach just to have a job. He taught us how to listen, how to learn, and how to apply what was taught. He would always make sure we understood before he would move on. I am now forty-four years old and I still remember this man!"

—CYNTHIA, MOTHER, CANADA

MY THERAPIST'S OFFICE

We all need to learn how to be alone, and it can be one of the hardest lessons of all. In the months after I broke up with my last—and only—serious partner (many, *many* years ago), I was in a very dark place. And I had to go through it to come out into the light. The comedian Louis CK, whom I adore, has a routine about this. He talks about how he's learned to just accept the fact that human beings sometimes experience real loneliness, and to let that sadness wash over him: "When you let yourself feel sad, your body has antibodies—it has happiness that comes rushing in to meet the sadness. So I was grateful to feel sad, and then I met it with true, profound happiness."

He's so right. If you are genuinely suffering, you're like a long-distance runner. After a while, the endorphins kick in, and you come out the other side stronger.

The designer L'Wren Scott, who had been a judge on *Project Runway*, took her own life in 2014. I was horrified, and surprised. She was the warmest, loveliest person, and gave those of us on the show who knew her casually no inkling that she was in turmoil.

One of the leading morning shows wanted me to come in and talk about her death, and to specifically address the evils of the fashion industry and how it destroys people. I wouldn't do it. You can't pin something like that on an industry, just as you can't pin it on another person or even a specific incident or circumstance. You never know what demons are in a person. Having attempted suicide myself with pills as a teenager, I know that such an impulse comes from a very, very dark place, unreachable by love or logic. There is no "reason" why someone commits suicide. No one thinking rationally could do such a horrible, permanent thing. When someone does, all we can do is be thankful for the time we had with that person and remind ourselves to take care of one another as best we can.

When I was a teenager, I was despondent when my suicide attempt was unsuccessful. I'm so glad now, though, that I failed. At the time, I was inconsolable and saw nothing but continued gloom before me. I wanted very much to die, and I resisted all efforts people made to get through to me. I avoided offers of help from my family, my teachers, and various doctors, until I met a therapist who essentially saved my life. He resisted all my efforts to put him off, all my acting out, and all my games. He just stuck around. No one else had ever done that with me. I realized that I could trust him and rely on him, and that's when I was at last able to begin work on rebuilding my life.

I was in a residential treatment facility, a hospital for adolescents and young adults, for two years and three months. My mother lied and told everyone I was away at school and that they didn't allow breaks.

"Not even for Christmas or summer?" the neighbors would ask.

"No," my mother would say, rapidly changing the subject.

There were sixty patients in the whole place, on two floors. Each floor had two wings. There was a high school there, too, in which twenty of us were enrolled. Initially I thought the whole place was a hellhole. The first day I was hospitalized, it was Ash Wednesday and I didn't realize it. All these people were walking around with ashes on their foreheads. *Is this some kind of branding that they do?* I wondered. I didn't know what it meant, but I suspected that whatever it was, it wasn't good.

But after a certain amount of time, it's like the monkey house at the zoo: stay there long enough and it doesn't stink anymore. I gradually realized I was so lucky to be there.

"My favorite teacher was my German great-grandmother. I know she may not be the traditional version of teacher, but from her I learned how to cook, clean, and sew. I learned the importance of the little details and having high standards. In her eighties she would starch and iron sheets, use laundry bluing to whiten towels, and use nice china for young children. I learned how to do needlework from her and she would undo stitches. For some people, taking out my stitches would have seemed unkind, but she had a high standard and made me believe I could do anything. She would gently take out the stitches and explain how to start again. There was praise when you did a good job. She was definitely a 'practice makes perfect' type of teacher. My nana had high standards but she didn't make them unattainable. She believed in you and pushed you to try harder. I think those are the marks of a good teacher."

—HOLLY, RECRUITER, CALIFORNIA

It did take me a while to find the therapist I mentioned earlier. One told me things like: "You call your grandmother Gummy because she *sticks* to you?" This therapist made a gesture with her hands like she was pulling taffy.

"No," I said. I loved Gummy. She was wonderful. She came to dinner every Sunday, and she always brought me a book. I made it a goal to read the book before she came back the following week so I could talk to her about it. "I only called her Gummy," I explained, "because when I was a toddler I had trouble saying 'Grandma.'"

"I'm not so sure about that," this therapist replied knowingly.

I perceived that she had a crush on another of my doctors. They deserved each other. He was the *worst*. I was open in the beginning and actually tried to talk. But he would say, in between puffs on his pipe, "So what?" or "Who cares?" I would say, "Well, I thought it was important." He made me feel small and dismissed. It wasn't pretty. I thought, *Why bother saying anything, then?* I stopped talking completely.

Some of the other patients were there for suicide attempts or drug abuse or chronic depression and even severe autism. One was there because he was gay. It wasn't that long ago, a little more than forty years, and we've come so far that people don't even realize it, but the world was very different then. At that time you could smoke on airplanes and homosexuality was perceived to be something horrible that needed fixing. This boy at the hospital cried all the time and he missed his mother. He was tormented by his sexuality. He was the first person who I ever heard say out loud, "I'm homosexual," and wow, did he not make it look fun.

I felt a profound sadness for him. It was awful. Before I knew what I was, sexually, I knew what I wasn't. I definitely wasn't a heterosexual male, but I also was hesitant to believe that I was what that boy was. He suffered so much. And how could I possibly put on to myself a whole new dimension of suffering? Impossible. I had a fondness for him, but I also had a tremendous fear of getting too close to him. There would be times when the stormy clouds would part and he was in a good humor and he was eminently likable, but usually he was such a gloomy sad sack that he was hard to be around. *Who would invite that misery on himself?* I wondered. Seeing him like that made me repress my own feelings.

Dr. Philip Goldblatt was young, but he was already a tough-love guy. He was right out of residency, and I was one of his first patients. He was a newbie, and had a lot of energy. He wasn't about to give up. I was ready, willing, and (I thought) able to break him. I took pride in being unfixable. And he, like good teachers, raised the bar. He said, "You're capable of more. You're capable of engagement." He insisted that I have therapy once every day, Monday through Friday.

For the first three or four months, I would sit there and say nothing. I'd had two doctors before him who let me leave when I stonewalled them like that.

"Why are we still here?" I would ask Dr. Goldblatt when he rejected a similar course of action.

"Because this is our time together," he said simply. "You can use it however you like."

And then he waited for me to respond. He didn't let me leave and he didn't walk out, either. He would just sit with me. I was a pro at freezing him out. I didn't even fidget. I'd had a lot of experience hiding at home like a living statue, staying perfectly still and quiet so I wouldn't be found. And so that's what I did in those sessions. I just sat, silent and unmoving.

We went on like that for ten or twelve weeks. I do the math now and I realize it was about fifty to sixty hours that we sat like that in silence. It became clear to me that this could go on for years. My determination to break him never wavered.

Eventually, *he* broke *me*. One day, out of nowhere, I just started talking.

In the course of the treatment that followed, I went from being indifferent to being incredibly angry to feeling affection for that man that was totally unanticipated. It was a case of my realizing that he really cared. I think a good therapist is also a good teacher. A good therapist doesn't give you information as much as he or she gets you to discover what *you* need. That's how I feel about my work with the *Project Runway* designers. It's a lot like therapy. I'm there to help them extract what they need to do.

My parents came up once a month for their own sessions with Dr. Goldblatt, and I didn't see them for the first year and a half that I was there. When I finally saw my parents after our many months apart, I completely broke down. They completely broke down, too.

Then my mother went into a diatribe about how she couldn't believe that she was the one who ruined me and did all this damage.

"What are you talking about?" I asked. She was conjuring up what was happening in her own sessions with Dr. Goldblatt. In a lot of ways, it was a very Freudian place, which was typical of those times. My mother felt she was being demonized in the course of this treatment.

We were not alone for that reunion, thank God. But after that I didn't really want to see them again. And they were traumatized, too. The whole situation was probably at least as hard on them as it was on me.

"William Manion, my eighth and ninth grade English teacher, connected literature's soul to mine. Despite what many value as a 'dynamic' teacher, Mr. Manion was quiet, thoughtful, and understated. He listened. He took time to understand each of his students. And then he connected them with authors who spoke directly to their mind, heart, and soul. He made literature seem important, even essential, and worth studying. He made new ideas and perspectives exciting to explore."

—CHIP, MARKETING CONSULTANT, NORTH CAROLINA

When I came out to myself as gay at the age of twenty-two, I went back to see Dr. Goldblatt. He was the first person I came out to besides the man I'd fallen in love with. I found the stirring of these new feelings inside me to be wondrous, but also terrifying. It was all so new. So much of my work with Dr. Goldblatt had been about how I possessed no sexuality. Of course, I had been in tremendous denial.

So much of what we'd talked about had a profound resonance and I would play it back. But then I reached a new land that I didn't know. It was a whole new chapter. I felt a need to go back to Dr. Goldblatt to validate what was happening, and for him to say it was okay—that is, to validate me.

When I came out to him, he reacted by asking me questions about how it made me feel. He just let me talk. He never asked me to reflect upon the work we had done before. It was about the here and now. He was an exceptionally good and intuitive person in every way. I had the maturity of a gnat, and he had extraordinary patience. I recall leaving and getting on the train back to Washington and feeling so relieved. Every day I'm grateful that I got help when I needed it. A happy life is the result of successful collaborations like the one I had with Dr. Goldblatt. Life is not a solo act.

If you're in a crisis, as I was, please know that there's help available. The national suicide hotline number is 1-800-784-2433, and the number for the Trevor Project, which has an around-the-clock crisis hotline for lesbian, gay, bisexual, transgender, and questioning youth, is 1-866-4-U-TREVOR. No matter how rough things are, with the right help you can find a way to survive—and to discover the wonderful, meaningful life you were meant to live.

III

ASKING

OCRATES FIGURED IT OUT thousands of years ago. Generally speaking, the best teachers are the ones who ask
their students the most questions. We need to make our students think. We are not mother birds dropping worms into
their mouths. We are there to prod them into realizing things
on their own.

There is such a thing as being overprepared for a class.
You don't want to come in with all the answers. You want to
make your students work. You're a guide. You're a mentor and
a leader. You're not Google. I confess to young people when
I don't know the answer to something, and sometimes even
when I do but want them to find out for themselves: "That's a
good question. Go find out."

Asking is the most important stage of a critique. I always
pelt the designer with a thousand questions. A short list of
common ones: Do you think it's working? Do you have any
concerns about it? Who is going to wear this? Where is she
going? What is the price point? Why did you pick this color/
textile?

I also consider asking to be the core of my philosophy of life. I go through the world every day trying to learn more about everything and everyone around me. In and out of the classroom, questions are your best friend.

MEETING NEW PEOPLE

Listening is so critically important. It doesn't come naturally to me, but I have a terrible fear of failure. I know if I listen well, I'll be ahead of the game. If I slack off and am not completely attentive, I am anxiety ridden. I feel that I am at risk and vulnerable. For me, it's all about being 1,000 percent present. Part of being a teacher is helping everyone stay present. If I sense that someone is drifting off, I will call on individual students and say, "Summarize what we have been talking about for the last thirty minutes." Sometimes you have to put people on the spot to make sure they are paying full attention.

When I meet people, I try very hard to learn their names and commit them to memory. If you're not in the moment, you hear the name and then you can't remember what it was. I repeat names. When someone says, "Hi, I'm Collette," I say, "Hi, Collette, nice to meet you." That helps. Sometimes I still miss names or forget them, and whenever that happens, it's a wakeup call. Some people make excuses. "I'm terrible with names!" I hear that all the time. Why give up? Step up to the challenge and find a way to compensate.

"Mr. Hill taught me high school history. He loved to delve into the why of historical situations, understanding the people to understand the motivations behind historical events. I think good teachers need to have a balance: the passion for what they're teaching combined with the patience to read a student and realize that they may need to change methods to reach them. Sometimes subjects don't come naturally to people and a teacher needs to be flexible and creative to get all of their students on the same page."

—TAMMY, ENGINEER, VIRGINIA

Last Easter I was at the Met admiring their medieval collection. A woman kept walking back and forth and then came over and said, "Someone told me you're on television. Who are you?"

I told her I was on a show on Lifetime.

"Why should I know you?" she asked.

"I would never say that you should know me," I said. "I make no assumptions that anyone would know me."

"Do I want to know who you are?" she asked.

What kind of existential question is that?

"I don't think so," I said.

Then I heard her go back and tell her friend, "No, he's nobody."

I honestly don't expect anyone to know who I am, even if we've met before. And I do make a very great effort to remember names, but sometimes I forget, too. If I haven't talked to someone for months, I might not remember him or her out of context.

One day I was sitting in the lounge of a hotel in L.A. waiting for my room to be ready. I was on my iPad and had blinders on. Someone was repeatedly clearing her throat nearby. Finally I looked up. I said, "Oh, hello!" The woman looked very familiar, though I couldn't for the life of me recall her name.

"I thought you wouldn't recognize me!" she said. And she talked for a long while as if we were old friends.

Well, I didn't recognize her! I pretended I had, and listened very carefully. Finally, from the contextual clues of what she was talking about, I realized who she was—a women's magazine editor I'd encountered on several occasions in the past. But that was only after two solid minutes of panic. I wish she had said, "Hi! I don't know if you remember me. I'm [name]. We know each other from [how we know each other]." And then I would have said, "Of course I remember you!"

On the topic of not recognizing people, a number of years ago I was on the red carpet at the Oscars conducting interviews for NBC and the *Today* show. This experience predates my three seasons of being part of the official red carpet preshow for ABC, an experience that spoils you for any other flavor of show.

For NBC, I was confined to an eighteen-inch swath of real estate behind a plastic boxwood plant. A producer stood behind me to tell me the name of each approaching star. Well, I saw a mature woman approaching. She was stunning, rather voluptuous, and had a mane of blond hair. But who was she? Not hearing the producer's voice, I looked over my shoulder. Gone. No producer. Well, one must carry on. So I spoke to this still-anonymous actress and when she spoke back—omigod!— I realized that she was the French goddess Catherine Deneuve! In a way, the lack of preparation was a blessing. Had

I known in advance that She was approaching, I would have been in a puddle and rendered incapable of speech.

I would also like to say that I love meeting people who know how to carry on a conversation. Sometimes it's tricky. But as long as both parties are making an effort, it usually goes well. Whenever I meet someone new and am at a loss for words, I have a stock phrase: "It's so nice to meet you! What would you like me to know about you?" Personally, I love open-ended questions like that, because it lets the person say anything at all, from "I am a dog lover" to "I am a doctor" to "Nothing! Good-bye." It's happened!

Occasional misunderstandings are inevitable, of course. Once I was at a luncheon being held to discuss the intersection of fashion and technology. There were some interesting speakers, including the designer Norma Kamali, who was telling members of her generation that they had to be less stodgy and embrace newfangled things, like engineered textiles. I was seated at a table in between Tina Brown, who was then the editor-in-chief of *The New Yorker* magazine, and the actress Sylvia Miles.

Sylvia leaned over me to tell Tina she had some poetry that would be very appropriate for the Valentine's Day issue of *The New Yorker*.

Tina said tersely, in her British accent, "Come and gone."

"I said, I have Valentine's Day poetry!" Sylvia said more loudly.

"Come and gone," Tina repeated.

"I said," Sylvia shouted in a deafening voice, "I have PO-ETRY FOR THE VALENTINE'S ISSUE!"

"Come and gone," Tina repeated.

Sylvia turned to me, flustered, and asked, "Why does Tina keep saying, 'Come again'? Is she deaf?"

"She said, 'Come *and gone*,'" I replied.

"*Ohhh*," said Sylvia.

Teachers have to pay very close attention to their students at all times to minimize misunderstandings and to make sure they know exactly what's happening in their classrooms.

One friend of mine illustrates how differently engaged two teachers can be. Here is her tale of two parent-teacher conferences: at one, her son's science teacher struggled to remember who the boy even was. She tried to describe the different kinds of plants they were studying and forgot the name of one. She's clearly not fully engaged. If she's burned out, she should take a sabbatical.

In the meantime, my advice in that scenario is: fake it! Say the child is lovely. Make up a Latin name for the plant and I guarantee no one will challenge you. Do anything you have to not to appear that you aren't in control of your material and aren't engaged with your students. At another conference, her son's computer teacher described the work they were doing in the classroom. Then he offered one specific compliment: "Your son is so polite. You should be very proud of him." Then he said, "Do you have any questions?"

When in doubt, put it back on the other person. "What do you want your child to get out of this class?" "What has your child said about the material at home?" The parent will leave feeling heard and like you are on top of things, even if you have no idea who in the world their child is (which, if that is the case, you should take as a wakeup call!).

A chemistry professor wrote to me online and said that he'd always believed teaching requires one thing above all others: full human presence. "One cannot pretend that the only thing that matters is the content," he said. "If you do that, you look like an idiot. Instead, one must acknowledge that teaching and learning are both deeply human endeavors that require a lot of mistakes to get right. You have to acknowledge that your students may not want to grow up to be you, and you need to support them in that." Hear, hear.

"Mr. Boyle, my fifth grade teacher, was fabulous. The fifth grade teachers used Broadway musicals in the curriculum, teaching the libretto, playing the soundtracks, and creating art and writing assignments related to each show. The year culminated in a field trip to see a Broadway show. Each week, Mr. Boyle went to the wholesale market in Philadelphia to pick up fruit. We pulled wagons around the school, selling the fruit to raise funds for the trip. He was a fabulous teacher: encouraging, tough when he needed to be, and very kind. (I also had a bit of a crush on him.) In part, because of him, I worked for over twenty years in theater and dance."

—ANGELA, FIFTH GRADE TEACHER, ILLINOIS

ON THE TALK SHOW COUCH

Terry Gross interviewed me on her long-running NPR radio show, *Fresh Air*. I found myself telling her things I'd never told anyone, like about how I was in a psychiatric hospital for two years as a teenager in the wake of a serious suicide attempt. It was because she seemed genuinely interested and was so gentle and respectful. She would say things like, "I'm going to ask you a tough question now. You're under no obligation to answer it."

"I'm an open book," I said. "People come up to me and tell me the most disarming things. That suggests a level of trust that I feel I need to reciprocate."

That's why I genuinely enjoy doing interviews and being on talk shows . . . most of the time.

Not long ago I did a forty-five-minute-long interview. The interviewer asked if she could record it. I said, "Of course!" That was on a Wednesday. We had a pleasant talk, although I did feel that she was not paying all that much attention to my answers, and she kept talking about herself rather endlessly. She called me the following Saturday night at seven p.m. to say she was transcribing and the recorder didn't work and could we redo the whole thing? I only very rarely say no, but I said no to that.

I am disturbed when journalists aren't careful. Once I was working at Liz Claiborne and my boss thrust before me an interview I'd done with a magazine. "Now you're creative director?" he said. "There are eighteen creative directors in this company. I didn't know you were one of them."

I called the editor and pointed out that error along with several others. "It was recorded," she said. "You must have said this."

"Get the recording and find any of that!" I said. "I find it hard to believe I would make such major errors about myself in the course of a single conversation."

She put me off. Then she said, "Listen, it's not as if anyone's going to read this."

To this day, I'm shocked by that response. And it begs the question: If no one's going to read it, why did I do it?

When I was a cohost on the ABC daytime TV show *The Revolution*, I conducted occasional celebrity interviews. The most difficult one ever was Andie McDowell. It was like interviewing a stone. Was this against her will? It was so difficult and awkward. Those three minutes seemed like an eternity. She gave one-word answers. And there would be a hesitation. It wasn't as though she was thinking about the question. It was as though I had interrupted her train of thought.

To my surprise, my favorite interview was with Joan and Melissa Rivers. They were fun and funny and great sports. In an interview like that, you're having a dialogue. You have to listen and let whatever the other person says be the prompt for where you go next. A segment producer would always hold up a sign that said things like, "Ask her about her plastic surgery!"

I ignored them. It's about where the interview takes you, or it feels too arbitrary. If she wants to talk about her grandson, let her talk about her grandson. You need to intently listen.

I always say this in talk show pre-interviews, something to the effect of: "Wherever Jimmy Fallon wants to go, I'll follow."

"Miss Carolyn MacPhie, my fifth and sixth grade teacher at Mayfair Elementary School in Toledo, Ohio, was amazing! It was 1975–76 and the country was gearing up for the bicentennial. Instead of sitting in the classroom studying the history of the United States, each of us chose an event from our nation's founding and created a piece for a mural that was done in our school's library It took quite a bit of doing, but in the end we all came together and created our own little Sistine Chapel. We were free to experiment and encouraged to make our own plans. I went on to become a teacher. I think of this Christa McAuliffe quote when I think of the influence my former teachers had on me: 'I touch the future. I teach.'"

—TOM, PROFESSOR OF STUDIO ART, MICHIGAN

I am comfortable going wherever the person wants to take it. The wonderful *Will & Grace* actress Megan Mullally had a talk show briefly, and I'm convinced that the reason why it was short-lived was because it was scripted. I was given the script when I got there, and I thought: *Talk about being overly prepared. Who knows where this conversation will take us?* Well, she did. It began with me popping into her dressing room on camera to say, "Hey, Megan! How's it shakin'?"

Dutifully, I went in and said, "Hello, Megan! It's so nice to see you!"

"Stop! Cut!" she said, looking exasperated. "Do it again. That's not what's in the script."

"But as long as you have your introduction, who cares?" I asked her.

"I do," she said.

"I'm sorry, but I will not say, 'Hey, Megan! How's it shakin'?'"

While on Katie Couric's show, I noticed she didn't seem to listen to anything I said. There was no dialogue. She just kept going from question to question.

Conan O'Brien, Seth Meyers, Craig Ferguson, Jimmy Kimmel, all of them are great at keeping a conversation going. I adore Jimmy Fallon. He's smart and charming, and he always seems like he's having fun, which makes the people he's talking to have fun, too. And of course the grand pooh-bah is Oprah. During the commercial breaks, she keeps talking. She makes asides. She makes you feel special. The first time I was on the show, I was a wreck. She came into my dressing room as though we were siblings. She put me so at ease. It took the nervousness away.

When I was in L.A recently, I was on *The Soup* with Joel McHale. I hadn't seen him since we'd been on another talk show together. On that show, he was picking on an audience member for what he was wearing. "Don't you feel," I asked, "that you should engage with him first and find out why he's wearing this outfit?" I was quite terse, to be honest.

The producers said, "Joel loved it when you went after him."

"I was actually hoping no one remembered that!" I said. "I thought I was rude. But then again, I also thought he was."

I appeared on *The Soup* right after Justin Bieber was arrested. We had fun. The hilarious Nick Kroll was Future Bieber and I was Future-Future Bieber. I wore the wig and everything.

One of my favorite talk shows ever was *The Bonnie Hunt Show*. Being on that show was so much fun. It was like a great lunch date. I was very sad when it got canceled. Word on the street was it was canceled for being too mainstream and not edgy enough. This was right around the time Tyra Banks had had a woman with two vaginas on her talk show. Bonnie was very philosophical about it. "Well," she said, "not everyone can find a woman with two vaginas."

AROUND THE NEIGHBORHOOD

One of the best things you can do for yourself is to cultivate a real community wherever you are. Even when I'm not feeling my best, I go out of my way to be kind to those in my neighborhood—and not just out of some kind of altruism. I keep it constantly in mind that they have things to teach me, and that we need one another.

I recently heard about a man who, when he lived in Manhattan, every day he got on the city bus for his commute, he said a bright good morning to the bus driver and called him by name. He also started a little club in the back of the bus with some fellow commuters. Each morning, even though they all came from very different social groups and would not otherwise have been thrown together, on the bus they shared snacks and gossip.

The bus driver was very quiet and barely murmured a greeting or acknowledged this little party in the back of the bus each morning. But years later this man ran into the bus driver, who surprised him by saying, "You made my job more fun. I loved those mornings driving your breakfast group around." The more you engage, the more you will feel like part of your community. Everyone wins.

I love walking around the city. But I also am shocked by how little attention some people pay when walking around. We need to be mindful when driving and when walking. A lawyer once told me that there are a staggering number of pedestrian fatalities in New York City every year. And I was not totally surprised. There are people texting while they're crossing the street. Why don't people pay more attention?

Not only do I not want to die crossing an intersection, I also don't want to bump into anyone on the street or sidewalk or have them bump into me. You never know what that can trigger. Sometimes I see people fly into a rage when they're bumped into. "What's the matter with you? Watch where you're going!" I would just apologize and get out of the situation, but often you see things escalate. "Watch where *I'm* going? Watch where *you're* going!"

I also hate driving. I have an overwhelming, disabling belief that there's no reason why people need to follow the lanes and it's a free-for-all. I feel at risk by being behind the wheel of a car. And I'll add that I'm not that good a passenger, either. A good driver to me is a rare and wonderful thing. I feel very comfortable when one of my extra-responsible friends is driving, but otherwise I find it tough to relax. Learning to trust other people when it comes to driving is on my educational agenda!

"My favorite teacher was Miss Allen in the third grade at Echo Park in Los Angeles. It was in the early 1950s. Everyone was finger painting an image of their hands. I was doing a Jackson Pollock–like splatter painting. Miss Allen saw my work and said, 'Keep going.' She gave a little girl the pride to do what she wanted, not to follow the crowd. And to this day I use that technique in my art."

—CARMELITA, ARTIST

REGISTRATION DAY

Students since the beginning of time have complained about having to take certain core classes. For me, math was a constant struggle. I was fine through geometry and then I went off a cliff. Geometry is so visual, so that was what I did understand. But I now see how valuable math is even in creative disciplines. When you're sizing garments up and down, for example, it's useful to know algebra. And I'm glad I tried to stretch my mind around the discipline.

When I started at the Corcoran as an art student, I wanted to be a painter and had no intention of doing anything 3-D. I was forced to take a sculpture class. Before even signing up, I went to my advisor and said, "This isn't advancing the plot for me." But then, once in the class, I had an epiphany. I could better realize what's in my head working in three dimensions.

When I assumed charge of the fashion department, I had a lot of people over my shoulder. I'd never taught a fashion studio course. I'd taught 3-D design. And so I would bring some of the students' sketches to other professors for their thoughts. Often the teachers would say things like, "Ugh! That drawing is horrible! That kid can't draw."

I'd say, "It's a senior's work. Does he have other talents? Is there something deficient in the instruction? We can't just say he's a bad drawer. We need to find something else he can do, or find some way to teach him what he needs to know." And then I would discover some other talent. For example, many of the "bad drawers" turned out to be superb at technical drafting.

There are just some things you're not going to be good at no matter what, but I discovered there were so many more criteria to assess than what had previously been assessed and evaluated. The department had looked at the students' capabilities through a very precise lens. It's like a dog whistle. I started to be able to hear other noises. That proscription needed to go away. I always believe in looking for what is exceptional in a person. It helps to know what the student receives satisfaction from. And it's essential to not take it personally if what the student receives satisfaction from is not your class.

But I guess what I'm saying is when you're signing up for classes, it's good to be open to having your mind expanded. Engagement takes many forms, but at its heart is curiosity. Whenever I'm asked for advice, my first suggestion is: Take a risk! It's like the first time you have a new flavor—cilantro, say. Who doesn't think in that moment, *What the hell is this?* And then, from that point on, some of us want it with everything! If you'd been left on your own, you would never know that pleasure. Would you believe that once upon a time there was a stigma against lobster? It's what was eaten downstairs by the help. Who was that brave wealthy person who said, "I don't care that it's seen as low class. By God, I'm going to try it!"

Denim was a textile no one would have worn outside of a dude ranch until Claire McCardell brought it into the fashion arena in the 1950s. McCardell was nothing if not a risk taker, and her work earned her the cover of *Time* magazine.

I love new adventures, which is why I am especially fond of the *Project Runway* challenges that involve field trips. When we went to the butterfly sanctuary during Season 12, I grilled the people who worked there and was shocked by some of what they told me. Who knew some butterfly species live a whole year, while some only last a day? I noticed that the other person who was throwing himself into this kind of investigation was Bradon, and he ultimately won the challenge. The depth of knowledge he acquired informed his design in a way that put him on the top. Asking questions and learning new things is like stocking a pantry. The more ingredients you gather, the more dishes you can make.

"Mr. Thorne taught high school calculus. I had him as a student in Watsonville, CA, in the early 1980s. He was always available before class to help struggling students. His passion for math was contagious. He would find interesting ways to integrate math into practical applications to make it more relevant. If lots of kids showed up before class asking for help, he would make adjustments to reteach that lesson rather than plowing on. He respected the students, which in turn earned him the highest level of respect from us. It was like being taught by your favorite grandfather, and you never missed that 7:30 a.m. class, even as a tired teen!"

—HEIDI, PHILANTHROPIST, CALIFORNIA

TEACHER EVALUATIONS
(AND THE THREE TYPES OF BAD TEACHER)

We all have that memorably awful teacher. Mine was a little bodybuilding German with a strong accent, which made it even more comical that his teaching style was a bit fascistic. He would come over and look at your drawing and say, "No, the apple and the orange are too far apart. Look carefully at the still life."

And you'd say, "But this is a better composition."

He'd say, "Draw it like it is!"

I told my advisor, "This is ridiculous. I don't want to draw or think this way. This is damaging me."

"Get over it," my advisor said. "This is what he does. You'll get something out of it."

I was rather petulant and intractable during my student days, but at the same time, I didn't want to fail, so I persevered. And I felt grateful that I'd already had a number of great teachers by then so that I knew the way he taught was simply one of many models. If he had been the first fine art education experience I'd had, I never would have gone into it. What I loved about studying art was this sense of the world opening up, the rules loosening up, and the ability to explore what you see, and to realize that everyone's view is different.

Sometimes those bad experiences can be catalysts. You fight against it. "I won't let that be true!" I have friends who say that teachers—or bosses, or in particularly tragic examples, parents—telling them they were no good was what propelled them on to greatness. I appreciate the value of a good revenge fantasy. I had plenty of naysayers in my academic career. They did motivate me to prove them wrong. My senior review was quite glowing and wonderful with the exception of one professor who said, "I would rather look at the empty space these sculptures displace than at any of these objects. My advice to you: you should cut off the tops of these and turn them into pencil holders." Oy vey!

And yet, I don't recommend trying to crush someone's dream as a good teaching strategy. For every student you push forward, how many would you scare away from the field forever?

It's funny, though: I remember teachers who were nurturing and inviting and engaging. And then I remember teachers who were hugely off-putting and insulting, and then there are all those ones in between whom I don't remember at all. And I wonder, is it possible those nameless, faceless teachers who never made any impression at all despite our many months together are in fact the worst ones?

One theory I have is that so much of what we learn from our teachers has to do with how we feel around them. Do they make us feel confident, or do they make us feel insecure? Do we flourish in their classes or wither? Trying out each teacher's methods, we learn what works and what doesn't work for us. We bounce our beliefs off them. Teachers with weak, mushy personalities who are checked out don't give us this opportunity for identity construction. We try to bounce an idea off them and the idea just sinks into the muck.

Online, I did a little poll of people's least favorite teachers. I was amazed by how terrible some of these teachers were! I found the stories unsettling and depressing, and so I didn't want to share them in detail with you. But I did want to share the gist of what I heard. Nearly all of the bad teachers fell into one of these categories, which happily enough create the acronym BAD! (Have I mentioned how much I love acronyms?)

THE THREE TYPES OF BAD TEACHER

1. The Bully
Cruel, mocking, and imperious, the Bully teacher shows no consideration for students' feelings. These Bullies create resentment and misery in their students, set them up to fail, and often turn them off the class's subject for life.

2. The Authority Abuser
Inappropriate, unprofessional, and unsettling, the Authority Abuser plays favorites and acts in a manner unbecoming to someone in a position of authority. These teachers abuse their power and confuse their students.

3. The Drone

Boring, burnt out, and distracted, the Drone doesn't listen to students and doesn't adjust lessons to the students where they are. Their standards are insultingly low. These teachers might as well be YouTube videos for all the support and personal attention they give students.

Here's a story that a performing arts teacher recently told me online: "My theater teacher was mean-spirited and had a particular hatred for boys. She would embarrass me in front of the whole class. Nothing was good enough. She never came to class prepared. She would arrive late and then proceed to tell us about her coffee, which she would drink throughout the class. She would answer her cell phone during class, and leave early when she felt like it. Her lectures were hard to follow, as she would change her mind on different topics. We never knew what to write down or what was important, because it was always changing. She never put the work into any sort of framework or context. She turned a number of students off the subject. My passion for the subject was, thankfully, stronger than her, but it was a long year in her class."

Can you imagine? I find such stories appalling, but I should not be surprised. Everyone I know, including me, has stories about terrible teachers. But I don't want to dwell on such people, because they are the exception rather than the rule. And perhaps if we come to recognize and better appreciate and elevate the wonderful teachers around us, we can hasten the retirement of the bad ones!

"My favorite teacher was my college choir director, John Rose. I had taken over planning music for the masses as a freshman, but was also in the chapel choir. During my junior year, he offered his services as organist. We planned everything together, though more often than not, he let me take the lead. He treated me as a colleague. The chapel singers joined us for a special occasion late that year. A question arose and, in front of the whole group, John deferred to me. One of them asked him why. He told them that since I had been handling the responsibilities for the past three years, it was my decision to make. He could have so easily made the decision himself and no one would have questioned it. To have someone of his standing treat me as his equal was incredibly empowering. I learned so much from him about the music I wanted to perform and the person I wanted to be."

—JENNIFER, MARKETER, NEW JERSEY

MY SENIOR SHOW

One of the perks of attending the Corcoran was that work was chosen from among the seniors' projects for exhibition in three galleries of the museum—a lot of space. There was a curator from the museum making the decisions about what went in. When I found out which of my pieces the curator selected, I went to Bill and Rona, my senior teacher and advisor, and complained.

"This other piece is so much stronger," I said.

"You need to respect the eye of the curator," they told me. "It's not about your piece of work, it's about how it fits in with the show and the other things she's selected."

That was eminently sensible, but I was mad as hell. When the exhibit was being set up, I went in and took my piece. I thought, *Better that there's nothing here!* There was a lot of "You shouldn't have! You should have at least asked permission." I said, "It's easier to ask forgiveness than permission." (And if this sounds familiar: yes, I later had a student at Parsons do the same thing, pulling something from the final fashion show there. Karma!)

I didn't even go to graduation, either. My parents were upset. "You can go," I said. "I'm not." I won the art history award and something else, and I wasn't there to accept them. The school tried to call me. I didn't pick up. I was a brat. Upon reflection, it was all so stupid. And the only person I hurt was myself. If I hadn't been so stubborn, I could have had an exhibit up for a whole month at the Corcoran. Washington's still a small town. The gallery owners were not many. They were looking for new talent. It was stupid. There can be a downside to the training we get at art school: "This is all about you."

OUT IN NATURE

I don't get out into nature very often, unless you count Central and Riverside parks, but the two vacations I have taken in the past ten years have both been to the Catskill Mountains in upstate New York for the weekend. Even then, I worked on my books, but it was luxurious to do so outside of the city. I sleep so well there. The stream that runs by the place where I stay is like a narcotic. Once, when I returned from such a weekend, someone on set insisted I'd had plastic surgery during my stay because my face had relaxed so much. Traveling to the country: it's cheaper than Botox!

I love learning about birds and trees. The other day, I was walking with my wonderful niece, Wallace, through Central Park to the Metropolitan Museum of Art. And for the millionth time in the park, I passed a sign that read, simply, "Pinetum." I have never known what it meant, and on this particular day, when Wallace asked me for the definition, I decided I should finally find out. We googled it on my phone, and learned that it's an arboretum devoted to pines. What a lovely name for a small pine forest, we agreed. Now every time I see that sign,

I'm reminded of how grateful I am for glorious fall days with my niece, and for this world so full of new words and other things to learn.

I feel the same way when I am out in nature, where there is such infinite complexity it boggles the mind. One day on a walk in the country, a friend's son handed me a fossil he'd fished out of the stream. It had the faintest impression of a trilobite. Millions of years ago, trilobites dominated the entire earth. They were *the* creatures. One theory is there was a Vesuvius-like cataclysm that wiped them all out. They've now been found in clusters of millions where it's evident that they all came together and then, presto, were frozen in time. They dominated for more than a hundred million years, and we still have evidence of them. And when you come across things like that, it just puts everything else in perspective.

"Mrs. Bouchard was my fourth grade teacher. She had a natural calmness, which made me feel relaxed. I was very shy at that age and did not have self-confidence. She made learning fun by holding contests. I won the contest for naming continents projected on the chalkboard the fastest. My prize was a Christmas ornament that I still have to this day, and I'm fifty."
—LORI, ACCOUNTS PAYABLE ADMINISTRATOR, MICHIGAN

THE LIBRARY

The class I taught from 2001 to 2007 was a thirty-week senior course called Concept Development. Students would work toward understanding their personal point of view and put together a final portfolio that would accurately represent that point of view to the world. When I'd originally started teaching, I thought: *I need to do so much for these students!* Then over time I grew more comfortable as a teacher and mentor, and I started to think, *I'm undervaluing and underutilizing these students.* And so rather than just pelting them with information each week, I started to make them do more of the heavy lifting. I would know what I wanted to talk about, but I would assign independent research homework every week so that they would all show up with different points of departure.

One week the class's subject was called "Wit and Whimsy." I left it to them how they wanted to do the research. They could go to the library. They could go shopping and record their findings. They could note witty things they saw on the subway. They could stand in front of Parsons in the courtyard and selectively report on what they saw go by. They could report on what they saw on television. I'm all about removing excuses. If they said, "I couldn't do this, because of XYZ," I would scold them. The assignment was so broad that they could do anything that even remotely fit the theme.

I encouraged them to use the library. I encouraged them to spend time just walking up and down the aisles and pulling things out randomly, to look at videos and films, and use the picture collection. I told them to get a stack of publications and flip through them until something caught their eye. Thanks to a huge donation by the celebrated magazine editor Grace Mirabella, we had a wonderful trove of thousands of vintage fashion magazines.

I wanted my students to experience that wonderful moment of discovery—that "a-ha" moment. When you're digging for gold at a library, you don't know what you're going to find. You find things you didn't even know existed an hour beforehand. It's very exciting. Following trails around online can also be fruitful. I recently found a 1950s Claire McCardell dress pattern on eBay that is almost identical to the '70s wrap dress. I consider it the wrap-dress Holy Grail. But the Internet has its limits, because not everything is on there. Too many people think if it's not on Google, it's not real. No, just no one has written it down or scanned it in yet. You could be the first!

In my class, the results of these research assignments were almost always revelatory. On "Wit and Whimsy" day, one student came in having fallen in love with Schiaparelli. Another talked about the Islamic collection that Yves Saint Laurent did that he was so reviled for. Another mentioned the outrageous and often very funny designer Elizabeth Hawes, who paired a dress called Alimony with a cape called Misadventure. Another brought in copies of hilarious old Maidenform bra ads, like one in which a woman is at a baseball stadium throwing out an opening-day pitch wearing nothing on her upper half but a sturdy bra.

We had a wonderful discussion, and we all learned a lot. I was there to shepherd learning, and to encourage my students to be responsible citizens of the class. But I was not there to do the work for them. Furthermore, when you require that the students participate in the class in this manner, they feel significantly more invested in the success of their experience.

By November each year, the students would always become quite competitive with one another. Each student tried to outdo the rest of the class in terms of what they could find. I liked it a lot. One student on her winter break took a day off from her family vacation to Egypt to visit Alexandria and interview people working on the excavation of Cleopatra's palace. She brought back a lot of photographs and we all applauded her enthusiasm.

Of course, some students would complain that they couldn't find anything interesting and were "bored." The one thing that constantly perplexes me is people who say they're bored. How can that be, in a world so rich and mysterious? To be driven to know more about something is a great thing. I like that phrase, "Only boring people are bored." I am baffled that with all the wonder the world has to offer, anyone could ever feel boredom. And yet, to this day, one of the most common things I hear from young people is, "I'm not inspired! Where can I find inspiration?" I always tell them: everywhere! Just this past week, I was inspired by Diane von Furstenberg's apartment, James May's house made entirely out of Lego bricks, a walk through Central Park, the young people at the

Teen Design Fair, a friend's vintage coatdress . . . I don't want to sound banal, but almost anything inspires me.

I look to students to determine what each needs in order to feel inspiration. As a teacher, I found that the best and worst students in a class were always the two most difficult groups to teach. The middle was easy. The toughest students for me were the ones who were either way ahead of the pack or who were trailing behind. But that's the challenge: to spend each day modulating lessons so that each group moves forward— helping those who are a bit behind catch up, and those who are ahead get even more ahead.

"My favorite teacher was my eleventh grade chemistry teacher, Mr. Varner. I was a terrible chemistry student. My lab partner and I made a noxious-smelling fire out of two chemicals—and that was the least of the horrible things we did. Mr. Varner never got angry, never told us that we were no good at chemistry, and never made us feel stupid. He just made us try again. When I later learned that Mr. and Mrs. Varner had adopted a child only to have the birth mother take her back, I had even more respect for him. He had suffered so much and still went on. Now that I'm a music teacher, I want my students to have fun, explore how they can express themselves, and to make connections to all things in their lives."

—JULIE, MIDDLE SCHOOL BAND DIRECTOR, MARYLAND

I'm teased sometimes for how often on *Project Runway* I stand back and put my chin in my hand and stare at designs, but that's a huge part of mentoring: helping the designer do that combination of looking at the bigger picture, focusing on what you have to work with, and dreaming as big as possible.

A lot of teaching is asking questions and really listening to the answers. Sometimes that means just sitting there in silence. When I had to confront Ken Laurence in *Project Runway* Season 12 about some aggressive behavior, I asked him what was going on with him and then he stared at me sullenly for a very long time before answering. This was edited down to a few seconds, but it was actually *minutes*. Years of teaching taught me just to sit there and wait and to stare right back. Eventually, he responded and we were able to talk through the issues—to a point. He insisted he didn't need help with his anger management issues, or anything else, and that was his prerogative. I've learned the hard way that you can't want people to succeed more than they do. If they tell you they don't need help, you can't push it.

But every good student and teacher I've ever known has been quick to admit a need for support and guidance. Good students ask questions just like teachers do ("Is this dress going too Copacabana?") and they really listen to and consider the answers ("Not if your client is Carmen Miranda"). They are respectful but true to themselves. They stand up for what they're trying to do without being rigid and unwilling to consider other options.

When it comes to the more creative aspects of one's education—whether it's fashion, art, drama, or music—the answer isn't in the back of the book. Yes, practice is practice. But after that point, how does, say, a pianist become noteworthy? Generally it's because of a unique interpretation.

When I studied classical piano, which I did for twelve years, my heroes were Arthur Rubinstein, Vladimir Horowitz, and Van Cliburn. They could play the same piece so differently, even with sheet music. That's one of the most amazing things about teaching: when you see each student bring their own soul to an assignment, you see twenty different right answers.

THE BARNES COLLECTION

Do you know about the art collection of Alfred Barnes of Pennsylvania? Mr. Barnes in his lifetime collected an astonishing assortment of works, including 181 Renoir paintings and a number of paintings by Cézanne, de Chirico, Seurat, and Matisse. There are so many famous paintings it feels almost obscene, and they're all thrown together—Goya, Corot, Soutine, Demuth.

Barnes housed them in a special building in Merion, Pennsylvania, arranging them in counterintuitive groups a Rubens next to a Dürer, say; or a fifteenth-century crucifixion scene alongside a Picasso—often along with metalwork, like spoons and hinges. The juxtapositions are surprising and the volume of incredible artwork is humbling. The Barnes family's collection is the stuff of legends. Along the top of one wall, for example, there is a huge Matisse mural. Can you imagine having such a thing in your home?

Well, the first time I saw the collection was in the 1970s. The teacher who took me was Andrew Hudson, the head of the art history department at the Corcoran when I was a stu-

I love the Greek and Roman antiquities galleries. The collection is spectacular, and the way everything is installed I find mesmerizing. The museum utilizes so much natural light. I've become fascinated by the way Greek vases tell a story. In a way it's a chalice or a bowl that's also a book. I've always appreciated the beauty of these extraordinary objects and the rich Etruscan red in so many of them. But now I read them like stories.

When *Project Runway* wanted to film at the Getty Center in Los Angeles, The Weinstein Company said we'd already been to a museum and why did we want to go to another one? As if we'd reached our museum quota! The Getty collection is staggering. When the Getty Villa opened, the Getty Center didn't exist, and so all the paintings were in this ersatz European villa. The collection was discredited because of this supposedly tacky, fake installation. Now all the paintings are in the Getty Center, and the Villa houses a spectacular collection of works from the ancient worlds of Greece and Rome. But I learned that people at conferences still say to the curators with disdain, "Oh, you're from the *Villa*." So many treasures there were apparently stolen.

One of the best things you can do in the world is take a child through a museum for the first time. I once had a conversation with a tour guide who does that for sixty children a day. I imagined he would be the most actualized person on the planet, but he was actually complaining about the kids—how they were wild, how they didn't pay attention.

I'm sure that must get frustrating. While filming *Project Runway* Season 7, we were allowed to go behind the scenes to see garments from the Met's incredible collection of historic clothing. Harold Koda, curator-in-charge of the Costume In-

CLOTHES SHOPPING

Like many of us in New York, I don't have a garage or attic or basement, and so have limited storage. We need to practice good self-discipline. To clean out my closet, I have to get in a very particular mind-set. I can't just say, "Okay, even though I don't want to, today I'm cleaning out the closets in my spare bedroom." I have to possess the wherewithal and express goal of getting rid of stuff. There are always tough decisions to make, but I don't think I've ever regretted getting rid of anything. And a nice thing about my building is that there's a laundry room in which I can leave things. So if there's anything someone might want, I put it down there and when I look again later in the day, it's always gone. It's like there's an elf down there!

Recently I realized two shelves were being taken up with all the sheet music I'd had when I was a young person studying piano. I no longer own a piano. I probably never will again. I haven't played for forty years. I'm so rusty that even if I had a piano, that music would all be too advanced for me. In making decisions like this I am reminded of Roz Chast's book *Can't We*

tiqued the work of the young people whom I brought along. She was sublime and divine. She didn't have to open her mouth at all; she was just so confident and fully present. There is no better spokesperson for how cool math can be.

Like all good teachers, she is able to be fully in the moment when she's talking to a student, because she's genuinely curious about other people and the world. You never feel that her brain is elsewhere. The webisode has received several million hits so far, and I hope that at least a fraction of those who watched it were made aware of how important math is to a rich life, whatever your industry. Here's to girls and math, and to DVF!

ized it was a badge of courage and learned to accept it and now I realize that most people don't even notice it and those that do find it interesting and distinctive." Done. But no. In the end, what we shot didn't even air.

Someone interviewing me the other day said, "Does it get to be a drag to be *on* all the time?"

"No," I said, "but it's a responsibility. If you're going to sleepwalk through an event, you shouldn't go. You owe it to everyone to be present in the moment, to participate fully. Otherwise, don't go! Does some of it require a lot of acting? Yes!" We have to show up and shine.

When I'm shooting a TV show, I quite literally live the show. When we're shooting in Los Angeles, that's especially true, because there are no distractions for me there. When we shoot in New York, I live here, and so other aspects of my life that can carry on do. But in L.A., I stay a block from the set. I get there early, usually before the sun's up, and I leave late. I miss meals. I actually quite like it. There's no wavering on the purpose. There's no time to meet anyone for lunch or dinner. On *Under the Gunn*, I'm me and I'm Heidi, so I'm on camera full-time and there isn't a moment to relax. I'm a bit of a workaholic, so I actually enjoy the entire experience. I love feeling fully committed.

No one embodies this spirit of commitment better than Dolly Parton, who I was lucky enough to meet when I was on a daytime TV show called *The Revolution*. We went through her closet. It was heaven. Even if she's just meeting you for the first time, Dolly makes you feel like you go back decades. That is a woman who knows how to be on all the time, and she even seems to enjoy it.

Prior to taping, I was told to ask her about a rumor that

(I was reminded of a dinner party at which Whoopi Goldberg said that she had moved to a gated community in New Jersey to avoid geing recognized everywhere she went, and Bette Midler joked back that she preferred the strategy of waving her arms as if fighting off swarms of bees while screaming, "Get the fuck away! Get the fuck away!")

Andrea acted as if nothing negative had ever happened between us. She went on and said the show was a great experience. She was in some state of denial or had spun the story to be something very positive. I didn't think it was positive. The last day she was on the show, she spent three hours at a sewing machine trying to put a zipper in the back of a dress. I thought, *How can this be?* I thought, *Hand sew it!* It would take less time. That a sewing teacher would be the weakest one in the room at construction? Who would write that scenario? I wouldn't. My concern during the audition process was that she would be helping people too much. Well, that was an unfounded concern, to say the least.

One other note on the auditions: one of the questions I always ask is, "Who is your customer?" Well, at this last round, so many designers said, "She works at an art gallery!" My response: "There aren't enough art galleries in the world to employ all these art gallery assistants you're designing for. I think you're just looking for an excuse to make crazy clothes."

For the first episode of Season 13, we had eighteen designers to present to the judges. The judges met with three an hour. At the end of this arduous process, Heidi Klum asked me to come in and comment on their selections. There was an incredibly talented young woman in their "No" pile.

"Why did you get rid of her?" I asked. "She's fantastic."

Soon after, I was on the NPR radio quiz show *Wait Wait* . . . *Don't Tell Me!* They hit me with some rather difficult fashion questions, and I was very nervous that I would look like an idiot. Fortunately, I got two out of three right. One was about spray-on clothing at a 2011 London Fashion Week runway show. Another was about a recent accessories designer who used road kill. After correctly answering that question, I went on my diatribe against fur.

The comedian Mo Rocca said, "What about Davy Crockett?"

I said that fashion exists in a context. In his time, Davy Crockett was very fashionable. But if you saw him on the streets of New York today, what would you say?

The one question I didn't get right had to do with a thirties film projecting fashion in the year 2000. The question was: "Which of the following clothing predictions were made?" And then there were multiple choices.

I guessed it was skirts and dresses that allowed you to change the hem length depending on the current fashion. I said I thought it was a good idea. In the future, surely you would want only one garment that would take you from poolside to club, or day to night. The correct answer was aluminum clothes with a hat that had a light on it like a miner would wear for finding men. Who knew? Bill, the very kind announcer, thought that my answer was better than the real one, which was some consolation. And in any case, I happily still won for the person I was playing for, and she won the prize: an outgoing voice-mail message from radio personality Carl Kasell.

GOING DOWN TO THE RUNWAY

There were several designers on *Under the Gunn* Season 1 who had time-management issues. Isabelle Donola made me crazy. She's smart. She's talented. But she had a characteristic the likes of which I've never seen on *Project Runway* or in a class. I don't know if it was subconscious or intentional, but thirty minutes before I called time, she would start ripping her garment apart, literally.

"What are you doing?!" I would ask.

"I don't like it anymore," she would say.

Up until the last minute she would be redoing her model's hair and makeup, too. I thought, *Is this some kind of compulsion, where she can't let it go?* She stayed on the show way past the point when I would have kicked her off.

Camilla Castillo was another one. I was shocked when Mondo chose her. She seemed to me like the runt of the litter. When I told her she was out, she filibustered. She said she'd worked too hard. She planned to stay. I said, "No, you're not. You're out."

One thing I find extremely important in teaching is consis-

prepared enough for what we're expecting of you. It wouldn't be fair to you if we accept you and then subject you to expectations that you can't meet at this time.

In my experience, the most common reason for failure was stubbornness: *I'm going to do it my way.* Fine. Your way fails. You needed to listen and you didn't. I think the common denominator in all of my disappointments with students and *Runway* designers is when they're unconditionally stubborn. They won't let anything in. That's an issue. Always. It's not about "Do what I say," either. I am always perfectly willing to be argued with. Please, fight back! But I don't take kindly to being completely ignored.

I taught one particularly stubborn student in 2002. The first year of the collections, he embroidered on all his garments threads that looked like pubic hair, and he stitched them on exactly where you would find pubic hair.

"It provokes," I told him. "But does it provoke for the right reason? Is it not going to merely be perceived as a cry for attention? Your clothes have beautiful construction details. There is a real voice here. Until you get to the pubic embroidery. And then it becomes a joke." I also pointed out that the fact he was a male made it even more of a perception problem. It came off as kinky, and that made it antithetical to his otherwise classic American sportswear aesthetic.

I had Grace Mirabella meet with him. "You have the ability to do beautiful work," she told him, "and so you really should." She told him he was distracting the audience from what was otherwise excellent work. This student had the power to be extremely successful on every level, and I hated that he was making a joke of it. If he were doing edgy, bitter, punk, urban street clothing, then maybe it would have worked. But this gar-

I thought part of the issue was that some of the faculty smelled this remarkable success and wanted to get on the train. The semester ended with Julie Gilhart, the fashion director of Barneys at that time, buying their collection in its entirety right off the runway. They won 2002 Designer of the Year honors, and would go on to win countless accolades after graduating, including an astonishing five CFDA awards.

"My high school U.S. history teacher, Paul Storbeck, changed how I saw myself. I was an underachieving student, and came from a difficult home. Most of my teachers were critical of me for not working up to my potential. Mr. Storbeck had an intelligent sense of humor, which I connected to. Like most sixteen-year-olds, I did not love studying history. I didn't see the point. That was all in the past. Why bother with it? But Mr. Storbeck encouraged the positive things he saw in me (curiosity, intelligence, humor) and ignored my negative, off-putting qualities. I responded. I became a student. I began to see myself as smart more often than smart aleck. That teacher truly changed my life, and probably had no idea that he had."

—LISA, SOCIAL WORKER, WISCONSIN

---

3. Read books. Go to libraries! I found Elizabeth Hawes at a library. The difference between Google and museums is like the difference between a bookstore or library and Amazon. Amazon recommendations are great, but there's not the same serendipity that you find at a library or bookstore.

4. Travel. If you can't fly someplace exotic like Angkor Wat, walk around your immediate surroundings and see what you can learn about where you live. Did the family down the street get a new dog? Did a new restaurant open up? Explore your neighborhood as if you're a tourist.

5. Listen closely. Being a good student of the world means being curious about other people and learning to focus on them when they're talking. Ask questions. Look people in the eye and smile.

T.E.A.C.H. Book Clubs

DISCUSSION QUESTIONS FOR EVERYONE

I. Who was your favorite teacher ever? What made him or her so important to you?

II. Who was your least favorite teacher ever? Why did he or she disappoint you?

III. Name one thing you've taught someone else in your life. Maybe it was teaching your child to ride a bike, or a friend to stand up for herself. What did the experience teach you about effective teaching?

IV. Name one thing you've learned in your life that has meant

dent there. He was a fabulous, incredible guy. I worshipped him. He took us on various field trips, including this one out of D.C. to the Barnes Foundation.

But the Barnes was a quirky place. For one thing, the Barnes Foundation school had a very particular aesthetic that it taught. And for another, they forbade group visits. There were forty of us arriving from the Corcoran with Andrew in the lead. And so we needed to hatch a plan. We plotted it out over a period of a couple of months, during which we made our reservations by phone in staggered groups of two and three. So the suspense had been building. Some of us were thinking, *Andrew Hudson is exaggerating this. This seems crazy.* But he was not exaggerating at all. The whole place was indeed kind of crazy.

We hired a bus and went to Pennsylvania. Then we got off several blocks away from the Barnes mansion. At five- or seven-minute intervals we went in groups of two or three. We were lurking outside hoping not to be caught. "No one's come back yet," we whispered to one another. So there was an excitement and anxiety. "Will they let us in?" and also, "Will they let us stay?" We were given strict instructions that we could talk to our small group but not to acknowledge others in our larger group. Andrew would be there but not engaging with us. It was simultaneously stimulating to be there but also thrilling because we all felt like counterspies.

That was forty years ago but I still remember it vividly. I remember the rooms, the furniture, and the light coming through the windows. It was a grand house. And it was made more glorious by the fact that we felt like we were on a secret mission. All teaching should feel like that—that you're lucky to be there and having way more fun than expected.

The other day I took the train down to Pennsylvania with

Ada, my coauthor, to visit the collection again in its new home. Now it's housed in a new building in Philadelphia itself. The galleries were designed to replicate the original rooms of the mansion down to a sixteenth of an inch! At first, as we were walking through the rooms, I thought it seemed cult-y that they had so obsessively replicated the original house. And I found myself almost exhausted by all the crazy mashups of works on each wall. I couldn't fathom the mind of someone who thought, *Let's put this ancient Egyptian work down here and then throw a bunch of Renoirs up here and then in front of it we'll put a dresser with a little statue of a duck.* My curator mind started to explode. But then I just gave up and went with it, and that's when I started to have fun. The more I relaxed, the more I realized the house was born of a profound respect for the man and his idiosyncratic vision. And I realized what a truly unique museum going experience it is. I bought the catalog and Ada and I read it on the train back to New York, and we read a few articles about him online, and it helped us better appre ciate the man and his collection. It's so important to have the context to understand why it was done the way it was done.

Ada and I did, however, get the giggles over the sheer num- ber of Renoirs. He's not my favorite artist. And, wow, were there a lot of Renoirs at the Barnes. I wish more exposure to Renoir could have helped me appreciate him more, but the more I looked at them, the gaudier they seemed, like they should be in a Vegas hotel lobby.

I will say I've never been to a museum with as much secu- rity. It feels like a fortress. I've been to the White House five times, so I can say with authority that there are more checkpoints at the Barnes than at our president's home. It seems designed to be intimidating, and it works! It's also very expensive.

The museum has a big entrance hall. There you can breathe. As soon as you enter the galleries, you can't. So, in a manner of speaking, that big space allows you to inhale before you enter the rooms, where you can barely take a breath because it's all so close.

There are a great many rules. There is no photography allowed. You have to check big bags and umbrellas. You have to stay behind a line marked on the floor, which made it hard to read the attribution on the frames. Ada was making some notes with a pen. A guard came over and said, "We don't allow pens here," and handed her a pencil. Huh? We speculated that a pen mark could do permanent damage to a work of art, whereas a pencil mark could be erased.

The printed guides provided information on the hinges and the Matisses. And as at so many museums, there were docents leading student groups. Some of these tours are wonderful, and some I find grating. I don't pretend to know how best to teach young people about how to look at art, but often I overhear conversations about things like shapes rather than content: "Where's the triangle? Find the pyramid shape!"

If it were up to me, I think I would rather have them look at how several different artists handled the same subject, like a still life of fruit. Or we could talk about how an artist's eye evolved over time. I would say: There are three decades of Renoirs here. Let's look at them chronologically. How did his style change from this year to this year? It speaks more honestly to what an artist does than looking for a triangle does. I would say: "Mr. Barnes arranged these things very carefully. Why do you think he put this painting next to this one?"

Chances are good that children won't overintellectualize such questions but will give you a visceral response, which is often a good one.

Art education is vital. Children need to know that thousands of years' worth of art is out there for them to enjoy and appreciate. And that when they make art, whether it's a clay sculpture or a finger painting, they are part of that tradition of generation upon generation who felt they had something to share with the world. All those artists did, and our young people do, too.

"One of my favorite teachers was my junior high biology teacher Mr. Hilary Hercules Fish. He was a 'confirmed bachelor' with a dry wit. My best friend and I would hang out after school sometimes and water his plants. Once I was having a particularly bad day at school. A classmate who I'd had a crush on had called me a dog from a few rows behind me, ensuring that everyone in the vicinity had heard the insult. Mr. Fish greeted me that day by saying, 'Hello, Miss Milton. What a beautiful smile you have!' Boy, did I need to hear that on that particular day!"

—CHRISTY, RETIRED RETAIL SALESPERSON, CALIFORNIA

THE METROPOLITAN MUSEUM OF ART

I've been a member of the Met, as it's known, for twenty-six years now. I revisit the same things, and every time I find something new about them. It's interesting to see all the connective tissue when you go through a museum.

I just found a book about Cleopatra at the museum's gift shop,[1] and was flabbergasted. I didn't know the Ptolemies weren't Egyptian! They were Macedonian and rose to power and ruled Egypt for the last three hundred of the last three thousand years of the dynasties. I love learning things like that.

Last weekend I went to the Met and wandered through the European painting collection. El Greco's work from the late 1500s looks like it could have happened in the first half of the last century. I was reading the descriptive text, which acknowledged that he was an odd man out, with a limited following. I could see why. I'd walked by the same paintings dozens of times. But this visit struck me in the most profound way. He was so out of step. How did that happen? It was his discovery by Picasso that catapulted him into popularity.

stitute, had put together garments representing five or six eras. He spoke off camera to the designers and said, "You may look all you like, but please don't touch." Four designers immediately started grabbing the dresses. I almost slapped their hands in my haste to get them to behave.

So I had some compassion for the tour guide. And of course not every child on every trip is going to connect to the art. But if you open a portal for just one student a day out of the sixty, just think what you've done for that kid for the rest of his or her life. And if that doesn't happen to one person a day, then I blame the tour guide.

Sometimes people ask what I want to do when *Project Runway* ends. I tell them that to wish for anything would be such horrible hubris. I've been so lucky—to live in this country, in this city, with such a rich life and career. I wouldn't even dream of saying, "I wish I could do X." But the truth is, if I had a second or a third life, I wouldn't mind being a curatorial assistant at the Metropolitan Museum of Art. I'm there all the time anyway. Put me to work!

The wonderful thing about visiting a museum is discovery—being made aware of worlds and objects and historical contexts that enrich you and cause you to see the world in an enhanced way. There's something thrilling about that. It's the easiest catalyst for discovery and learning. The museum has done all the work of presenting it. All you have to do is open your eyes. And when you read the didactic text, you learn the background.

Recently I was sick for four days. I didn't make my bed that whole time, and when I don't make my bed, you know it's dire. On the fifth day I finally dragged myself out of my apartment to see a show of Charles James dresses at the Met. A friend met me there and we spent a long time looking at the dresses' construction and talking about how different they looked in person than in photos. And then we stumbled into another exhibit called *Lost Kingdoms*, which displayed hundreds of years' worth of beautiful art from Southeast Asia. There were peaceful Buddhas from the fifth through the eighth centuries!

Some of the pieces looked almost alive, and they were from a time and place that I knew almost nothing about before that moment. The beauty of the work made me want to learn more. Moments like that create a whole new path in your learning life. I feel so lucky to live in New York, where there's never a dearth of things to see. There are so many extraordinary museums, and the exhibitions are constantly changing.

"Mrs. Mary Bartlett, my private harp teacher for almost twenty years, inspired me to push myself when I was tired. She taught me to hear the music I didn't know I had inside myself. And she told me interesting stories about her life growing up to keep me entertained yet focused. I still hear her beside me when I'm learning a new piece or part of a score. Once in my midteens, practicing stopped being a priority. My schedule was: get up, go to school, come home, make a snack, watch *General Hospital*. 'Are you going to be a nurse or a harpist?' she asked. I got the message. I went back to practicing every day right after school."

—JANICE, FRENCH TEACHER, CANADA

PLAYING WITH LEGO BRICKS

As a kid, I loved making things. In particular, I loved building in three dimensions. As a toddler, I had cardboard building blocks, each the size of a shoebox. You could stack them. But you had to be careful, because they could fall over very easily and they could be ungainly.

When I discovered plastic Lego bricks, it was love at first sight. Among the many things I loved was that these bricks stayed together. You didn't feel that what you were making was so fragile. It wasn't a tenuous structure.

I was a kid when Lego bricks first came out, and there were no sets like you have today; no Lego Friends or Sydney Opera House or X-Wing Fighter. You could just do whatever you wanted with them. You were only limited by your imagination.

I was always building houses. At that time, there weren't even any roof tiles or windows, or even lintels for over the doors or windows. I just left door and window holes. Sometimes I improvised little doors with cardboard. And I made zigzag rooftops, as you would an Aztec ziggurat. I still remember how ecstatic I was when windows came out. And then doors! With hinges!

When the kits of prescribed designs came out, that was all I could ever find to buy. I wanted to just get a box of plain bricks, but I could only find sets. And so I bought some for my nephew and encouraged him to just build anything he dreamed of. He was not impressed. We would pour the contents out on a tabletop. I was eager to see him dive in and explore, but he was fixated by the image on the box and would become frustrated if he couldn't exactly replicate it.

"But this photo on the box is only one thing you could do!" I would say. "You need to be creative. Think: if you could build anything in the world, what would it be?"

"Creative is not good," he replied, looking uncomfortable.

I went straight to my sister and said, "What is going on in this school of his?"

I was very concerned that he wasn't being encouraged to think outside the box, and sure enough, that was the case.

"They don't like it when students color outside the lines," my sister said. "Trees have to be green and bark has to be brown and the sky has to be blue." There was a discouragement of creative thinking, and it had shaped him into the Lego-averse child I saw before me. I found it tragic.

Then I met Ada's son, Oliver, who is now seven. For the past three years, abetted by Uncle Tim, he has been a Lego obsessive. He is intuitive enough and confident enough to know that the box cover is only one example of what's possible.

He will complete a set I give him in about five minutes, let it sit in his room for a week or so, and then take it apart and combine it with all his other bricks to build something new and fantastical. To be blunt, Oliver is a Lego prodigy. The other day while at Ada's apartment working on this very book, I saw that Oliver had created a two-foot-tall model of a museum that incorporated elements of his models of the Hogwarts castle, United Nations building, and Chima characters. He's blazing new trails!

"My sixth grade teacher had been a nurse before she became a teacher. The science part of our class included a biology section. I was entranced by the miracle of the human body. She recognized that and gave me special projects to work on. I decided then and there to become a doctor. This was quite unusual for an eleven-year-old girl in 1966! I have loved my thirty-two-year career in medicine and it's not over yet. That teacher took a little extra time to encourage my interest and it made a huge difference in my life."

—SUSAN, COLLEGE HEALTH PHYSICIAN, KENTUCKY

Talk About Something More Pleasant?, which was very inspiring to me. She writes about moving her parents into assisted living. Their apartment full of stuff stopped being charming and nostalgic once she had to deal with all of it.

When you do head out to shop, I believe you shouldn't be a blank slate open to whatever presents itself. You should have the inventory of your closet in your head. Taking stock of what you have and what you like to wear is key. If I have a pair of pants I haven't worn for three years, I need to ask myself why.

While I think it's fine to impulsively buy something, I don't think it's a good regular practice. We can end up amassing things we didn't want that much. I'm susceptible when I'm shopping online. I now practice the self-discipline to not buy it the same day. I put it in my cart and then return the following day. If it's still pulling at my heartstrings, I get it. Four times out of five, the next day I've changed my mind.

Which brings me to another commandment: you must try things on. I don't care how many layers of clothing you're wearing or if you have a child in a stroller or you're in a rush, don't buy something without trying it on. I've been in so many closets where there are items with tags still on them.

"It doesn't fit," is invariably the refrain.

"Why don't you take it back?" I ask.

"Because it's too late."

It makes me feel sick. What a waste!

You should be in constant dialogue with your closet. Do you have shoes to match every dress you own? New York is a blessing in a way, because we live in smaller spaces than much of the rest of the nation, and that helps us think about our clothes with an editing eye. I'm so self-disciplined because I know I'm a hair shy of being a hoarder. I'm serious. It's an inclination that needs to be beaten back.

The only things I let proliferate are books. I've built lots of sturdy bookshelves. Let the books keep coming! But I am ardent about weeding through magazines. Invariably, they're online, and so there's no reason to save them. With clothing or objects, if something comes in, something has to go. When I shop, I think, *What will this replace?* It's not good for your clothing to cram things into a closet. When you try to extract something and fifteen other items come with it, it's time to pare down. To succumb to the instinct to hoard is to give up. We must never give up!

Whenever you go out to shop, you should have certain items in mind as a goal to find. You shouldn't feel a need to compromise on style or budget. You should feel ready to walk away with nothing. It's not a waste of time if you don't buy anything. You're learning about what's out there, and you're getting a better sense of what you like and don't like. It's important to have a heightened degree of self-awareness when you shop. You can hold something up and ask, "Is this me?" If the answer is no, walk away! The retail industry may be pushing something—like pink capri pants—but you don't have to accept that.

The fashion industry does not always make it easy on people who are especially tiny or large. For example, if you talk about women beyond a size 12, they act like it's tarnishing the brand. If you asked most women, they would celebrate it! But I'm heartened to see some designers beginning to push back. For her shows, Diane von Furstenberg insists on no underage models, no eating disorders, and no limb-lengthening surgeries. And her wrap dresses fit practically everyone. I've always said I wished *Project Runway* would do a season using only models size 12 and above and other nonconventional-model shapes—short, blocky, petite, everything!—so that the designers would have to design for the kinds of real women actually living in America.

I don't believe in buying aspirational clothes. They will languish in your closet. Buy things you can wear now, not that might fit you after you lose weight, or once you feel better about your arms, or whatever. Pay attention to silhouette, proportion, and fit. Never assume that anything will automatically fit you properly right off the rack. You may need to have things altered, which is easier and cheaper than most people realize. Most cleaners and tailors will fit garments to you for a nominal fee, and you will look instantly so much more pulled together.

On the topic of age appropriateness, no one ever has to look dowdy. Women will often tell me, "I'm in my fifties. I'm supposed to look dowdy!" No, you're not! You're also not supposed to look like a hooker. But you don't have to be a church lady. Every time you go shopping, you should try on as much as you possibly can to learn more about your body and what makes you feel the most like yourself.

"My high school French teacher truly believed in his students. You wanted to make him so proud. His motto was, 'The world becomes a smaller place with each language you learn.' I carry that with me thirty years later and went on to major in languages in college and graduate school. I travel the world and use my languages daily. Knowledge really is power."

—CATHERINE, NEW YORK

IV

CHEERLEADING

T HIS IS THE POINT of the critique in which I say, "You can do it! Go, go, go!" One of our most important jobs as teachers is to support our students in whatever it is they want to do, even if it's not what we would do ourselves. As soon as a student enters our class, we must do everything we can to support that student and to make him or her feel believed in and appreciated. It is so depressing when teachers badmouth their students. I always hated to hear complaints in the faculty lounge about how lazy or useless a group of students was.

I'd work with people who would say after the first day of class, "These few students are going to be great. These other ones are going to flop." I'd say, "Really? That can be a self-fulfilling prophecy." At some point, that burden is on you as a teacher. I similarly cringe when a person complains about how all the people he or she is dating are "terrible in bed." Really? What's the common denominator among all those students, and all those dates? *You*. Maybe you need to take some responsibility for your own experience of those other people.

DINNERS OUT

I go out a lot for work, and sometimes I get to meet wonderful people. (The other night, I was so starstruck by Gloria Steinem. She was absolutely charming.) But other times I am at events that go on hours past it seems like they should, and I am in rooms full of people with whom it is a struggle to engage. What makes such a thing fun? The most fundamental thing imaginable: being with people who are comfortable talking and who seem to be happy to be with you. It's no fun to be with someone who doesn't know how to have a conversation, or with someone who seems unhappy to be there.

I do a lot of charity lunches, meaning people bid and "win" me, and I take them out to a nice lunch. For one, I was early for the lunch and thought I would just look around the gift shop at the high-end department store where we were meeting. I saw a rather peculiar-looking person and thought, *Who is that? What a shifty-looking, odd, Peter Lorre character.* And it turned out he was the one I had to have lunch with. *Oh no, it's the Peter Lorre character!* And I wasn't wrong to be wary. One of the first things he said to me was that he could smell my cheap suit across the table. Can you imagine?

Neither do I enjoy ice princesses, those who are too guarded to ever connect with you. It's refreshing to find someone who's living life and who's ready for fun wherever they go, like Diane von Furstenberg, who's always looking for an adventure and is always tremendously engaging.

One thing I would like to add about eating out: I believe in tipping as much as you can possibly tip. I have great respect for anyone in service. I want to show my appreciation. Unless someone does something egregious, I feel it is my duty to be as generous as humanly possible. It's not that I'm "buying love," as my mother always called high-tipping. This isn't someone I will ever see again, in all likelihood. But as long as I can afford to do it, I don't see why I wouldn't go out of my way to surprise someone with an extra twenty or however many dollars. As long as I can do it, I will. I feel that I've done the right thing, and I hope a small windfall might make a small difference in someone's day. It's win-win.

ON VACATION

I haven't been on a pure vacation since 2001, when my niece, Wallace, and I went to Paris for a week. She was fourteen. We went all over the city and took an excursion to Versailles, too. We had a wonderful time.

When my niece and nephew were young, we went to Disney World. I loved it. They have the most marvelous way of anticipating what you want. I even liked waiting in line. The anticipation builds. As an adult, not even speaking for Wallace and Mac, I was never disappointed. I never once thought, *Why did we wait in this line?* It always paid off.

And I loved how all the "cast members" treated people. Once my friend saw an angry woman try to fight with a cashier there. It was hilarious. Everything this grouch said to antagonize the worker met with no resistance. Nothing stuck. "I was supposed to get fruit with my breakfast!" the woman said. "Oh, I'm afraid it's not included with that breakfast," the cast member said, "but you go ahead and take a fruit if you'd like one! It's on me! Take two!" And the woman just spluttered, totally frustrated that she couldn't get any traction on her rage. That's one of the wonderful things about taking the high road: it disarms people.

Whenever I travel, I want to go somewhere where I will learn something new. People tell me they consider that the antithesis of what a vacation should be. "You should go to the beach and be a vegetable!" I'm told. But that doesn't appeal to me. I'd like to go somewhere that challenges my thinking and makes me see the world afresh. I am desperate to see Angkor Wat, for example, in Cambodia. The Khmer Empire lasted from 802 AD to the fourteenth century. It was a city of about a million people. The ruins of their great temples are now in the middle of a jungle and farmland. How incredible would it be to stand there now?

I'm reminded of the great children's book *A Street Through Time*, which shows one place over the course of thousands of years—from when it was a farming village, to when it was part of the Roman Empire, when it was attacked by Huns, when it went through the industrial age, right up to the present day. It makes you conscious that we are part of the human race, a very tiny point on a very long line that stretches backward and forward through time.

"My favorite teacher was Debbie West, my junior high choir teacher. Moving back to the States from a military base overseas, I found public school a complete culture shock. I was painfully shy and insecure. Ms. West made me feel safe and visible. She nurtured my musical talent while helping me find my own voice. It's been more than twenty years since I sat in her class, but her voice still plays in my head."
—REBECCA, SINGER AND STAY-AT-HOME MOM, VIRGINIA

SHOOTING A SCHOLASTIC WEBISODE

Forgive me if I get on another soapbox for a moment. The ranks of girls studying math and science are appallingly low. The teenage daughter of a dear friend of mine is a very zealous and ambitious math whiz named Robin. As an extracurricular project, Robin partnered with Billy DiMichele, vice president of corporate productions and creative services for Scholastic, the largest independent content provider to schools grades K–12, to create and produce a webisode called "Math@Work: Math Meets Fashion." Robin's mother asked me whether I would agree to host it. Of course!

Robin and Billy presented a rundown of the various locations and content for the webisode, including visiting a fashion designer and having a conversation in his or her studio. Would I help recruit designers? Of course! Frankly, I didn't believe that we needed to look any further than Diane von Furstenberg, but her name didn't conjure instant enthusiasm in anyone other than me.

"We need someone better known to our audience and with a young and hip vibe," said Robin.

Better known than DVF? That's impossible. But I complied. I was successful getting some younger designers to take my calls, but upon revealing the purpose of our video conversation, the response was universally the same: "Math? Eek! No!"

What's wrong with these people? I asked myself. How can anyone be active in any design discipline and not engage with math on a daily basis? To be honest, these math-fearing designers sounded rather ignorant, which disturbed me enormously, because they were playing directly into a stereotype of fashion designers that persists in the academic world. (I was constantly battling that stereotype during my time as chair of fashion at Parsons.)

Robin's mother, my friend Liz, is extremely well-connected. She suggested that we approach a merchant rather than a designer, and suggested Mickey Drexler, the genius who led Gap, Banana Republic, and Old Navy to ubiquity and then took over J.Crew and set its trajectory in motion.

I have the greatest respect for Mickey, but young and hip? He's even older than I am. If he and I were to be on screen together, the K–12 audience for the webisode would think that we taped it in an old folks' home. Forget it.

I began my DVF campaign anew. She has tons of worldly experience, created a fashion staple with the wrap dress, and herself is a fashion icon. She's president of the Council of Fashion Designers of America, *and* she studied economics at the University of Geneva in Switzerland. Does anyone possess better credentials than that? Oh, and did I forget to mention that she's a woman, too? This webisode was intended to speak to girls.

Well, I was victorious. DVF it was! Not only did she agree to participate, she opened up her studio to us and warmly cri-

AT THE MOVIES

Films about the education system are frequently annoying to me. Everyone loved *Waiting for Superman*, that movie about how charter schools will save the world, but I found it annoying. I thought it oversimplified the idea of educational opportunity and made the process seem alienating.

Most movies about teachers, too, are just plain silly Often the teacher is portrayed as either a god or a fool. The teacher as superhero, entering a broken school and waving a magic wand over it in the form of tough love, is a false concept. Without the help of, at the very least, his or her students, even the best teacher can't create an ideal learning environment.

Nor is the teacher-as-buffoon realistic. Very few people graduate from college and become certified without at least some reason for going into the profession. Unless the administration is asleep at the switch, how could more than a very few total duds even make it into the classroom? Such depictions are not realistic, and not kind. I far prefer subtler depictions of teaching. Here are some of my favorites:

"I've had a lot of really awesome teachers over the years; all the way from day care to college. One of the most memorable was a professor in college who taught church history (I know, it doesn't seem promising but it was great). He had traveled all over, so he talked about places and times as if he knew them. One day, he came to class dressed up as a monk. He then proceeded to give a lecture on Peter Abelard in the first person. It was mesmerizing! Now that I'm a teacher, I look back on that and try to make my lessons interesting and relevant in any way possible. Many different types of people can be good teachers but the most important qualities are passion and compassion."

—STEPHANIE, ESL TEACHER, CONNECTICUT

Up the Down Staircase (1967)

There was a time when Sandy Dennis starred in *everything*. In 1967, she was on the cover of *Time* magazine! Well, in this film she stars as a teacher at a rough school. I thought it was well written and well acted. She has a tremendous amount of empathy. She has a soft spot for these kids. She is determined to help be part of the solution. There's a very moving scene where a student is in love with her very pretentious English teacher. She writes him a love note and he hands it back to her with the grammar corrected. She has a horrible reaction, as one would. Well, Sandy Dennis consoles the student and bitch-slaps the teacher, as well she should.

Desk Set (1957)

Written by the Ephrons (Nora's parents), this film is not necessarily about teaching, but it is about how to do excellent research and to convey that information clearly to those who need it. Katharine Hepburn runs the research department for a major television network. Spencer Tracy comes in to install a gigantic computer. It's a quasi-romance that never culminates. Their relationship is extremely funny. Hepburn and her team outsmart the computer and it blows up when asked a question that's too hard. Her superpower is a broad scope of general knowledge and a keen sense of where information is hiding.

The Prime of Miss Jean Brodie (1969)

Maggie Smith is incredible as a life-loving teacher at a strict girls' school. She plays favorites and takes "her" girls on outings to the country, to the opera, and to look at art. She is passionate about teaching, and yet she has a serious down side. She's a classic example of a teacher for whom there is only one way to look at things· her way. She unintentionally scars one student, who retaliates by getting her fired.

The Harry Potter movies (2001–11)

Maggie Smith again! She plays Professor Minerva McGonagall, the strict but savvy teacher of transfiguration at Hogwarts. McGonagall has firm boundaries, although she will once in a blue moon bend the rules, such as to let slide Harry's rule breaking in order to increase the Gryffindors' chance of winning at Quidditch. One thing I love about the Harry Potter series of books and films is the nuance of teacher-student relationships. Harry and his friends have a number of teachers whom they love, others whom they hate, and plenty to whom they are fairly indifferent. What strikes home is how often such feelings change over time. Snape is redeemed. Dumbledore seems to Harry as a god, then as a fool, and then as something in between, which is what, ultimately, we all are.

TAPING *GUIDE TO STYLE*

I once had a TV show called *Tim Gunn's Guide to Style*, on which we did makeovers. We would bring in experts to help make over women with certain issues. Once we had Padma Lakshmi on to talk to our client about a scar she was trying to come to terms with. Padma has a scar on her arm from a childhood accident. The intention of the show was to help the woman own it, to think of it as a badge of survival and not to be ashamed or embarrassed. Padma came in late, surrounded by an entourage. Because we were far behind schedule, the producer tried to get her on camera right away.

"I haven't had hair and makeup yet," she said. So we got her into hair and makeup, and then we took her to meet the woman. She looked at the woman's leg and seemed taken aback. She didn't do the coaching we hoped she would. I had to pick up our woman's morale afterward because she was in a state of, *Why did that happen?*

All Padma was supposed to do was share her own experience. I felt that I could have done it: "I felt like you. I thought my scar was horrible and would scare people away. But I real-

when she goes camping with her husband of close to fifty years (yes, Dolly goes camping) she does so incognito; that is, sans hair and makeup.

"Are you kidding?" she said. "I wear full hair and makeup to *bed*! What if there was a fire in the middle of the night? I wouldn't want to disappoint the firemen!"

Bless her.

"My high school art teacher, Teresa Staley, has always been my inspiration. She was kind but always pushed us to try new things and to keep editing our work. She advised us that failure was as important as success if you learned from it—good advice I have taken to heart."
—CATHY, PUBLIC SCHOOL ART TEACHER, INDIANA

PROJECT RUNWAY AUDITIONS

Every season, about a month before we start shooting, we do a nationwide search for the next group of designers to compete on *Project Runway*. We look at the work of hundreds of people and ask them questions about their work and their lives. The goal is to find people who have the talent and the character required to make it through the grueling competition. The whole show shoots in a month. Every show you see is just one or two days. Speaking for all of us involved, we have almost no breaks or free time. It tests the strongest of constitutions. And weaknesses of ability or creativity are discovered very quickly once the shooting starts.

I'm always very nervous at the auditions. My nervousness is driven by truly not knowing what's about to walk through the door. We do have paperwork on these designers, but one of these people is going to be the winner. Is the person coming in next going to take it all?

I feel my role there is to be a truth teller about the design talent and that part doesn't make me nervous. I have enough experience to know when someone's work is adequate or not for the show. Then I ask, is it exciting or not? Then, what is this person like? How do they interact with us? I'm so invested in the show and I only want the best, but I also have to tell myself, someone is going to be the first person out. I want to have the confidence that anyone we pick could win the whole show.

We're looking for designers, not dressmakers. I frequently meet designers and think, *These clothes are beautifully made, but I see nothing innovative. This may keep you on the show for the first couple of challenges, but then the judges are going to ask, "Where's the excitement?"*

Then you have those who have ideas for days, but no skill. Then you have the scammers, who bring work they haven't even done. Or they misrepresent themselves in some other way.

At the Season 13 auditions in L.A., I met a designer whose work was excellent. He had been to design school and seemed very bright. I began talking to him about his work and mentioned the renowned American dress designer Claire Mc-Cardell, my all-time favorite fashion person. I adore her 1956 book, *What Shall I Wear?* And I was so pleased when it was rereleased in 2012. The case could be made that there would not be an American design industry without her.

I should say now that I am very patriotic. I believe that all American designers should educate themselves about the proud tradition of post–World War II American fashion. Alas, few do. Once I overheard a prominent designer say at the Council of Fashion Designers of America, "I don't consider myself an American designer."

Can you even say that if you're getting a national design award?

Anyway, back to the auditions: this young designer looked quizzical when I mentioned Claire McCardell. "Do you not know who McCardell is?" I asked him.

"No," he said.

"You just went from here to there for me," I said, holding my hand above my head and then toward the floor. "How can you not know the history of what you're doing? You're referencing work that you don't even know about."

Not to mention, I took a tiny bit of personal offense, because not long ago I published a history of Western fashion in which I talked about McCardell ad nauseum. Maybe you'd say it would have been brownnosing for him to read my book in preparation to meet me, but I say, brownnose away! It's better than being unprepared.

Another one of the excellent people we met with expressed ambivalence about being part of the industry. I said to her, "I'm woeful about your potential, in that case. I don't disrespect your opinion. But if that's really how you feel, you shouldn't do this. I hate when people quit. That's the worst thing that can happen. And you sound like a candidate for quitting."

We can't have a potential quitter on the show. It's not only a morale issue for the remaining designers and for the audience, but it also screws up the eliminations. We have to say to the judges, "You can't eliminate anyone this week." And that's terrible! What if someone crashes and burns that week and we have to keep them just because this other designer bailed out? It's bad for everyone.

And it has happened. Who remembers Andrea Katz from Season 10, the sewing teacher who after being up for elimination then sneaked out in the middle of the night? It's one thing to struggle with being on the show, but to bolt like that, with no good-byes? That shows such poor qualities of character. I ran into her on the street one day. This voice called out to me on Broadway. I turned and looked. She approached me in such a way that suggested we were the best of friends and cheer-fully told me that she had been enjoying the experience of being recognized on the street.

"Mrs. Patricia Pregitzer taught our high school's 'early bird' classes. These were classes like Genetics and Human Be-havior that couldn't fit within the normal school day, so she offered them at 6:30 a.m. What teenagers would take such classes? As it turned out, quite a few of us. Mrs. Pregitzer was due to retire when I was a ninth grader, but my friends and I begged her to stay until we graduated, and she did. Our last year was her last year. She understood that kids from a tiny rural town in western Michigan had little enough going for them, and she could make life better by preparing us for college and life, even if that meant we all had to come to school two hours early. By sheer force of will, she inspired us to move up, move out, and move on. I remember the day in class when she fixed her stare on me and said, 'You're going to the Big U (the University of Michigan) and getting your Ph.D. and you're going to make something of yourself.' It hadn't occurred to me. She saw it. She made it seem like a done deal. I did go to the Big U and did get my Ph.D. And now I have my dream job, talking with the brightest students in the country about the fundamental nature of the universe. And they pay me for this! I dedicated my PhD thesis to Mrs. Pregitzer. It seemed like the least I could do."

—ALAN, CHEMISTRY PROFESSOR, CALIFORNIA

"Because she's so *derivative*," Nina Garcia said. "When I see her, I think Gareth Pugh and Rick Owens."

Pugh and Owens—for those who don't know, and there's no reason you would—are two successful young designers who make work with a vaguely knight-like aesthetic. Before I did the research for *Tim Gunn's Fashion Bible*, my 2012 sweeping history of Western fashion, I might have let such a thing slide, but no longer.

"I'm sorry, but that's such a limited way of looking at it," I said to Nina. "I look at her work and I think she, Owens, and Pugh all harken back to the arms and armor of the Middle Ages. I don't say that she is only who she is because of Rick Owens. They all are who they are because of King Arthur."

Nina seemed disarmed, and I was so happy when she moved the designer into the "Yes" pile.

Alas, I couldn't save everyone I liked, although I did try. One piece of advice I gave all of the designers before their meeting with the judges was, "If the judges aren't saying anything right away, don't step in and fill the void with your voice. Let the silence breathe. If they ask you a question, answer it succinctly, and then wait. Don't just start babbling. Generally speaking, if the judges are quiet, it means they're thinking. Let them think."

Most of the designers took my advice and had good meetings. But two of the designers to whom the judges responded most unfavorably were babblers.

Learning to be quiet when you need to be is vital. It's hard to listen to silence, but in so many areas of life—job interviews, dating, therapy, the classroom—it is a wonderful thing to be able to sit in silence and just listen, even if it takes the other person a little while to get around to what they need to say.

"My favorite teachers were a married-couple teaching team who provided a safe space for their music students. Whether to hide from P.E. or rehearse for a show, we always had a safe place to be in school during those difficult teenage years. Now that I'm a teacher myself, I think of them and try to cultivate an environment where everyone is excited to learn."

—ROBERT, PERFORMING ARTS TEACHER, CHINA

COMPETING ON
HOLLYWOOD GAME NIGHT

Recently I was asked to be on the NBC quiz show *Hollywood Game Night*. Well, if I'm on there, then obviously "Hollywood" should be in quotes. I suggested they use this line in their ads: "*Hollywood Game Night*: Who are these people?"

Well, I was terrified that I would embarrass myself, so I did a lot of homework before being on the show. When I was teaching, my students always kept me current. Today I still find I learn things from young people. When I hosted the D.C. Teen Design Fair, I thought, this is a good opportunity to learn about social media. I was surprised to learn that their favorite app was Instagram. Facebook took too long to scroll through, they said, and they totally shrugged off Twitter. I would never have guessed that.

So, too, when I was teaching, these popular-culture people would be their muses, and they would talk about a show or a band that was inspiring them and I would check it out. But now I'm out of the loop on a lot of popular culture. So I went out and bought *People* magazine and *OK* and a few others. I memorized as much as I could about celebrity couples and scandals. I felt as prepared as could be.

Jane Lynch of *Glee* hosts, and I love her. She's hilarious and fun. Onstage, they have a bar. They want you to drink. I had a glass of champagne. Well, many of the other players started hitting the bar hard. One was drinking tequila on the rocks, and I thought, *Uh-oh.*

Sure enough, she got wasted and kept flirting with the *Survivor* host Jeff Probst and sitting on his lap. At one point, one of my fellow players, David Alan Grier, said, "Stay over on that couch!" Because she was so tipsy, she couldn't do anything for our team. At another point she almost fell in the fireplace and I yelled, "This is unsafe!" I'm always the party pooper. "At least someone is being sensible," Jane said when I apologized for being a nag.

David Alan Grier is quite funny, but on the show he was hugely competitive, to the point that he didn't have a sense of humor about it. But he kept the conversation going backstage. He asked the producers and P.A.'s questions like, "Who's the dumbest person you've ever had on the show?" They were very diplomatic, and said, "No one's been dumb. Some people have been difficult." "Oh!" he asked. "Who's been the most difficult?" "I shouldn't say," said one of them. Another said, "I'll say! Padma Lakshmi." When I watched her episode, I found her to be terrifyingly good at the game. She was out for blood. But she was so competitive, she even dominated her own teammates. I thought, *Don't you know they're on your side?*

I felt like we had to keep our wits about us, because the game is quite hard. There are two teams of four. You have to hit a buzzer. Well, we drew a rough bunch of questions. Two rounds in, not one of us had answered a single question correctly.

"Jane," I said during the break, "this show is a lot of fun to watch. At the same time, I'm finding it quite difficult. Have you ever had two rounds as hard as these two?" She said no. It's possible she was just trying to make me feel better, but I think they were actually extra tough.

Well, things got slightly better after that. What we had to do was look at a picture that was two celebrity faces merged via Photoshop. They told us one person's first name was the same as the other person's last name. And then we had to figure out the names. "We have too many synapses working!" I said. I got one right. The first clue was "J. Lo's ex." And then there was a long pause. And the second clue was "Hannibal Lecter." It was Marc Anthony Hopkins. And in the end, our team did win. We won $25,000 for our player. We worked hard for it!

"My seventh and eighth grade science teacher, Mr. Beye, was always a fun and entertaining teacher. He was also a volunteer first responder. A month into my freshman year of high school, I was involved in a very bad car accident along with two classmates. I was hospitalized for five weeks. While I was in the hospital, Mr. Beye came to visit. I had my jaw wired shut. He walked in just as I was midway through trying to suck pudding between my teeth. I had it all over my chin. After cleaning it up, he talked to me about school. He suddenly stopped and became very serious. He said it was the scariest thing to pull up to such a bad scene and find out three of his previous students were involved. There were tears in his eyes. Until that day, I never realized a teacher could care about their students that way."

—VICKI, STAY-AT-HOME MOM, KANSAS

"Mr. William Ferrell was hands down my favorite teacher. I was his theater student for four years at Apollo High in Glendale, AZ. During that time he taught me a lot about theater and stagecraft. He taught me that I was important, what I had to say was important, and that I could make a difference. He taught me to be creative and to fight for the right to be a creative person. He taught me to be responsible, how to work with others, and to solve seemingly unsolvable problems. He taught me the meaning of dedication, the reward for hard work, and the joy of living a life dedicated to something I loved. He taught me to love myself, embrace my flaws, and to be humble about my successes. He gave me the freedom to fail and the opportunity to learn from that failure. He gave an odd, dorky young girl a chance to flourish and find success. I will never forget this man. He literally made me what I am today."

—CONNIE, HIGH SCHOOL THEATER TEACHER, ALABAMA

V

HOPING FOR THE BEST

To WRAP UP THIS book, I'd like to now talk about how to let go. It can be the hardest thing in the world. Designers don't want to declare a garment done. Parents don't want their kids to leave home. Mentors don't want to admit that the ultimate outcome is out of their hands, that they've done all they can and have to cross their fingers and hope it will all work out well for this person in whom they've invested so much time and energy. The people we teach become repositories for our fondest hopes, and it can be hard to watch them stroll off into an uncertain future. The last thing I do in a critique is to tell the designer or student, "You're free now! Good luck!"

It's how I feel when I've participated in makeovers. If you can inscribe in the participants what they should be doing to be responsible citizens of the world and look their best, at least they know what you think they should do. It's up to them whether they actually do it or not. This can be the hardest lesson. But it's crucial. We need to let people go and do what they're going to do without taking it personally. When they come back and tell us we've helped them, we can feel proud, but either way we can feel like we did our best.

After taping *Guide to Style*, I would frequently be asked about doing a "where are they now" follow-up show to see how well these makeovers had stuck. My response: I'm not even remotely interested, because these remarkable women know what to do to look their best, so it's their decision whether they subscribe to those guidelines or not. I'm not a fashion policeman. And I never will be.

tency. If the paper is due on Friday, the paper is due on Friday. We need to be very explicit about what is and isn't grounds for postponing a deadline. Will we accept a doctor's note? Will we accept the paper a day late in exchange for the loss of a certain number of points? Any solution is fine so long as it's been arranged in advance and does not change randomly.

One easy way to infuriate a student who's worked hard to get something in on time is to then say to other students that it doesn't matter and turning it in the following week is fine. You can have almost any rules you want, but leaving deadlines and boundaries fuzzy is a recipe for disaster. Not to mention, that's not how the real world works, so what fantasy world are you preparing your students for if you don't enforce limits?

"My favorite teacher was a man named Bob Grothe. He was the man who inspired me to become a teacher. His enthusiasm for English and theater were apparent to anyone who met him, and his dedication to his job was unlike any other teacher I had met. He believed in challenging his students, expecting the best we could do, and pushing us to achieve. His passion and caring made him emotional. That humanity kept him a real person in our eyes. He was the only teacher who ever went out of his way to talk to my parents, to give them a cold hard dose of reality and tell them to get over themselves and their divorce and to take care of my brother and me. As a teacher I've tried to make sure my classroom became a place where students felt valued."

—JACLYN, FORMER HIGH SCHOOL ENGLISH TEACHER, ILLINOIS

DISCIPLINARY HEARINGS

Teachers tell me that students are constantly plagiarizing work from the Internet. As we know, it hurts them the most. (How much do you learn from that beyond how to cut and paste in Word?) But it also hurts the other students, who are working hard for their grades and having to compete with Wikipedia.

When I had students who copied, I took it very seriously. I threw out one student for plagiarism in the spring semester of his senior year. It was painful for me to do that to him, but I felt like I had no other choice once I learned that all year he hadn't presented any original work.

For some time, his fellow students had been telling me he was turning in other people's work, but I thought it was jealousy and immaturity talking. Finally, though, I felt there were enough complaints that I needed to investigate. I went to his faculty.

"Are you aware that your students have come to me saying this student is not turning in his own work?"

"Oh, he's such a good boy!" one of them said. "He's very busy."

"Wait, aren't you shocked by this accusation?" I asked.

"We thought everyone knew," one said.

They were covering up for him!

I couldn't fire them, because the union was there by that point, but I did write them up and reported them to the union. I challenged their grades. I said, "It's not fair to the students who are working hard. It's not fair to him to let this drift by. Why aren't you outraged and insulted? It's a slap in your face."

Well, the student went on to great fame. Obviously, cheaters do sometimes win. But that doesn't make it right.

One related problem I see in teachers and curators sometimes is historical revisionism: presenting the facts in a skewed way to suit their own agenda. Educationally, I find it immoral. For example, in the 1970s, Anne Truitt was lecturing on twentieth-century sculpture and made a sweeping statement that took me aback: "David Smith was the first twentieth-century sculptor to paint his work." I thought, *Really?* She was a grande dame, and so I wasn't about to challenge her in front of the class, but I went up afterward and asked her if she meant that statement.

"What about Calder?" I said.

"But I don't like Calder," she said with a quizzical expression. "Do you?"

She just knowingly removed him from her treatise. I wish she'd said: "Calder was the first, but I don't like him, so I'm going to talk about David Smith." As a teacher, you have an obligation to provide the facts, even if you don't like them. You can present it in a leading way, the way lawyers do in a courtroom. You can sway your audience, but don't misinform them!

"Mrs. Sweeney, my first grade teacher, discovered that I could read already, and encouraged my ability and creativity, not worrying about 'grade level' constraints. Curiosity and an eagerness to learn can be instilled at an early age."
—BEVERLY, KINDERGARTEN TEACHER, NEW JERSEY

GIVING FINAL GRADES

When I was teaching at Parsons, if I gave a student an F, Student Affairs would descend, and say, "What did you do?!" To me! As if I was the one who'd received the F. "The student only came to three classes, and didn't turn in any assignments," I would say. "What was I supposed to do? Move into his dorm room and hold a gun to his head until he did the work?"

Sometimes it is your fault as a teacher, and it's worth doing some self-exploration: Did I not give the student adequate opportunities to prove himself? Was the way I delivered the content too hard to assimilate?

But usually it's not your failure. It's the student's. If you've done the introspection and feel that it wasn't your fault, you need to forgive yourself. You shouldn't feel responsible if sometimes a student just doesn't get it. Some of the students may not have the aptitude. It's okay. We will all survive if someone fails. And, in fact, it may be a great gift. It's only when we bomb totally at something that we find the other thing that we're meant to do. It's what I said to those who we rejected at Parsons: it's not that we don't value you, it's that you're not

ment wasn't going into a gallery. The assignment was to create something that might sell. Who's going to buy this? For me, it always came down to the question: Who is your client? I am fairly sure that Mrs. Obama is not going to wear a pubic-hair-embroidered skirt.

"My favorite teacher was Peter Thompson (drawing and painting, University of Kansas). I would be surprised if he didn't make a strong connection with every student who ever walked into one of his classrooms. Everybody loved him. I always got the feeling he genuinely loved teaching and truly cared about each of his students. I think his special talent was that the metaphors he used to talk about making art could meaningfully be applied to life in general."

—DARCI, HOMEMAKER AND ARTIST, KANSAS

That same year, twin Russian international students collaborated on an homage to September 11. They had foam-core towers toppling. All the mannequins and models had halos and wings. They also wanted to have a fog machine. No joke. I told them, "It's too soon, and it's in egregiously bad taste, ladies."

"It's a political statement," they said.

What is the statement there? Is it, "These people are dead and I'm having them model my clothes?" That's not a statement. That's just macabre and offensive.

They did it anyway. The jury of selection voted them out of the final show.

One student had fantastic 1960s modish color-blocked clothes. They were ahead of their time, because that look hadn't come back yet. But in the show, from which the jurors were choosing who would be in the final show, her clothes were installed in what looked like something out of *Pee-wee's Playhouse*. I said, "I don't know where the clothes stop and the props start. People are going to walk right by."

The jurors universally hated it. It was impossible to extract what was what. Often this kind of thing comes from a lack of confidence. They don't have faith in the clothes, so they cover them up with gimmicks.

Another student was the only one of the seventy who refused to use a fit model all year. We had fit models in the studios all day every Tuesday and Thursday. Those were the construction studio days. This student refused to put anything on anyone. I was walking through the show with designer Yeohlee Tang. From thirty feet away, with no editorial input from me, she pointed at the clothes and said, "That collection has never walked." Stunned, I looked at her and I said, "You're right! Those clothes have been on dress forms all year." "I can tell," she said. I told the student right away. You can't fool some people. One of my refrains to her faculty was, "What happens when these clothes do get on someone?" It was a nonissue, because she didn't make it into the show.

To everyone who was not in the final show, I made this announcement: "You're not in the show. It's not because your work was conceptually problematic, although in some cases it was. It's not that it was poorly made, although in some cases it was. It's not that it was poorly installed, although in some cases it was. There is one common theme: stubbornness. That was your downfall. You need to listen to feedback, especially if there's a consistency to it."

When teachers brag about their students' success, I tend

to raise my eyebrows. Do I believe you were an ingredient in their success? I'd like to. But I also find it unseemly whenever teachers act as though a successful student couldn't have done it on his or her own. In my experience, most designers are going to make it regardless of what we do—unless we derail them.

"My biology teacher, Mrs. Aiken, was very quirky. Her eyes were different colors. It was rumored she had been struck by lightning twice. One of her fingers was crooked. And her homework was impossible to get right. But I loved her. She would give us extra credit assignments, and even though I didn't need the points, I did every one, including scraping a dead animal off the road so I could label the bones. She understood the weird kids and was probably the only teacher who ever understood me."

—WHITNEY, HOMEMAKER, GEORGIA

When I started on *Runway*, I was so afraid that a designer's bad critique on the runway was my own. I fretted. I felt guilty. How could I have not saved them from the mistakes they made?

Eventually I realized I'm there as a catalyst and a prod, but it's not up to me what they do, or whether or not they take any advice I might give. If they ask for my opinion, I will give it. But they live or die by their own decisions. I constantly tell them that they have to accept responsibility for their own work.

It was liberating. How do you gauge their success if you put it on yourself? Especially when it's so hard to predict what will work and what won't. Early on, I could anticipate with good accuracy what each of the judges would say. And then, in Season 8, I started calling them "the crack-smoking judges."

We talked about this on *Under the Gunn*. You can't say that the success of the designer or the failure of the designer is inextricable from the mentor. By definition, someone's going home. It's musical chairs. It's not as though we only get rid of a designer if he or she fails egregiously. That's one of the reasons I told Nick that he had to stop doing *any* work on his designers' looks. It's not Nick's failure if one of his designers goes home. However, if Nick is doing all the designer's sketching and creating all the design work and directing hair and makeup, then it *is* on him when the designer goes home.

When Mondo was asked to comment during his designers' runway critiques, he often said, "We did this," or "We did that."

"What's this 'we' business?" I asked.

He said, "That's what my mentor said." I said, "It makes the line between you and your designers fuzzy. The line needs to be crystal clear." There's nothing wrong with saying, "This designer decided to do X. She believes in it. As her mentor, I support her. She knew you would either love it or hate it, and I encouraged her to take that risk." As a judge, that context—a daring risk—makes me more excited about the work. I'd rather have you be on the edge than be safe.

When I was asked in the workroom whether I believed the judges would like something, I would say, "Who knows? I can't pretend to guess what the judges are going to say." That also was liberating. I'm able to say with impunity, as long as you feel confident that this is the best you could do under these circumstances, then what more could you ask for?

AWARDS CEREMONIES

Some great designers came though Parsons when I was there, and there were those who benefited most by being given free rein. In general, teachers need to say the following to their students: "You tell me what you want to do." It's not about telling them what they can and can't do. So often those kinds of things come from professional jealousy. Whenever I see a teacher try to hold back those who are ascending quickly, I try to say, "Don't hold on to them. They might crash and burn, but you have to let them try."

On *Under the Gunn*, Sam told me that his teachers at Parsons, where he studied, told him he would never be anything other than a ready-to-wear designer. When he made a genuinely beautiful, original garment, I would tell him, "This is a giant fuck-you to those teachers who told you that you were only a ready-to-wear designer."

At Parsons, this was true of the two young men who would become the wildly successful design team we now know as Proenza Schouler, a.k.a. Lazaro Hernandez and Jack Mc-Collough. Their senior year started out rocky. They weren't coming to class or completing work. I actually filled out their withdrawal forms. I said, "Sign these forms if you're not going to be here." But in speaking to them, I learned that they were too enthralled in this collaboration with each other to do their other individual work, and they begged to be able to focus on collaborating. I gave them permission.

Well, some of the faculty went nuts. They accused me of enabling them by allowing them to collaborate. They were furious with me. They thought it was a gay thing, and always referred to the three of us as, "Oh, *you* and those *boys*." Jack and Lazaro were a couple then. They lived together. But they were in different sections. "Those boys are lazy bums!" one teacher told me. "Don't invest in them!" The faculty hated me. It didn't matter, because I was only concerned with what was best for the students. I let them do a portfolio together and a collaborative collection. I said, "This is the first year we're letting students make collections. This is a new day. The industry is collaborative. Let's let them work together. What is this industry if not collaborative? This could be a great precedent for other design teams." If each student needs five to seven looks, they'll have ten or fourteen. They ended up with twelve.

Throughout the term, I checked in on them, and I was very pleased by what I saw. The "boys" were pushing each other's work beyond what either could do alone. Their work was phenomenal. I saw the collection in muslin in January. It took my breath away. The nuances. Asymmetrical collars. How they were playing with hem lengths. It was innovative without being crazy. It was visually captivating. It was stimulating. Then the faculty swooped in to try to control the fabrics. "Up to this point there has not been a misstep here," I told their teachers. "They know what they're doing. Leave them alone!"

SCHOOL VISITS

One of my favorite things in the world to do is to visit schools. Recently I had the honor to speak to the parents of students at P.G. Chambers School, an extraordinary northern New Jersey K–12 school for children with physical and psychological disabilities.

The classes were incredible, each geared toward the students' specific needs. Some students, for example, had sight but their brain jumbled the information, and so classes took this into account and presented information in ways their brains could comprehend. Class lessons were generally no more than fifteen minutes long, owing to their brief attention spans. They broke up an hour of reading into four sections. The students were in a constant state of excitement, and I was bowled over. There's freedom and agility to respond to what the students need. P.G. Chambers School does what works.

The teachers help the students with practical skills, such as how to grocery shop. They project shopping lessons on a large screen. They also have a kitchen, in which they make snacks to sell every Friday. They take the profits from these sales and invest them back into ingredients for the next week. There's competition for who's making the most delicious dishes, and who's being the most frugal. This teaches real-life skills in a fun way.

Many students were in wheelchairs or on crutches. I don't know when I've felt so overcome with emotion. Not since being at Walter Reed National Military Medical Center did I have such a feeling of humility and hope. I looked around and thought, *This should be stressful and depressing. But instead it is a place of utter joy.*

Those kids are so remarkable. They help one another. The teachers give their support, and the teaching assistants demonstrate a most remarkable commitment to a positive and challenging educational environment. And when I was there, they were preparing for a 5K race! I was blown away.

When I was on the tour of the school, spending time with some of the students, I was told that some luminaries who had spoken there before had turned down the tour, afraid it would be too unpleasant. They didn't want to see the kids. But that's why I wanted to go. I wanted to see and interact with them. And I did. They were so loving, and so enthusiastic. Many of them knew me from either *Project Runway* or *Sofia the First*, and so we were able to talk about those shows and, more important, about what they were learning. One mother had twins there, a boy and a girl. How do you deal with the hardship of having not one but two severely disabled children? But you do. You just do.

Peter Crimi, a remarkable individual who spoke to the parents' association before I did, has cerebral palsy. He is a graduate of the school. He had gone on to Rutgers and returned as a faculty member. He was impaired, but extremely commanding

and eloquent, and in possession of wonderful leadership qualities. He gave a beautiful talk. Well, that didn't help me at all. I
got up to speak and promptly burst into tears.

Immediately, I was afraid they would feel these were tears
of pity, so I clarified as soon as I was able to calm down. "I'm
so sorry," I said. "I wear my emotions on my sleeve. And I want
you to know that I'm not crying because I feel sad for you or
feel sorry for these students or some kind of there-but-for-the-
grace-of-God relief. What I feel is a supreme privilege that
I am allowed to bear witness to the triumph of the human
spirit."

There was so much love and happiness in that room. I can't
even think back on it without crying. I'm a better person for
having been there. It reminded me of what education is all
about: a place where abilities are celebrated and issues are
addressed, where people young and old work together to learn
and grow. May each and every one of us have such educational
opportunities for teaching and learning in every aspect of our
lives.

TAKEAWAYS

Five Fast Ways to Learn Something New Right Now

1. Love your work. Learn new things about and find ways to enjoy whatever you do for a living, whether it's cleaning bathrooms or managing a company. In one of my favorite children's book series, Mrs. Piggle-Wiggle, the clever Mrs. Piggle-Wiggle finds ways to get children to enjoy chores. For example, she teaches one girl to pretend a wicked witch is going to inspect her dish drainer in ten minutes, so she has to rush to get all the dishes done before the clock strikes noon. We all need an internal Mrs. Piggle-Wiggle to find ways to enjoy the parts of our jobs that aren't fun.

2. Go to a museum! Take every opportunity to discover things you don't know exist. I encourage rampant googling, too, but when you google, you only find information you search for. When you look around a museum, things find you. What treasures are waiting for you? Return to the same museums again and again and marvel at how much you missed the first time around. Realize everything in your life is like this.

something to you. Maybe it was learning to drive or how to read or how to close a big deal at work. What did the experience teach you about being a good student?

V. What could you do today to reward good teachers? Maybe it's sending a letter to your child's principal praising an especially good teacher at the school, or calling your brother to thank him for teaching you to ride a motorcycle, or writing an email to a college professor who meant a lot to you about how you recently reread a book she recommended. Good teachers never receive enough recognition for the work they do. You can help change that!

DISCUSSION QUESTIONS FOR TEACHERS

I. Who made you want to become a teacher? Where is he or she today?

II. Who have your favorite students been? Who were your most difficult students? Were any of your favorite students difficult? Where are they today?

III. Do you have a script in your head of what you're trying to do when you teach? I'll give an example. For me, it's the T.E.A.C.H. model, which breaks down roughly to this script:

> **T:** *Here's what I see happening.*
> **E:** *What are you trying to do?*
> **A:** *What do you see happening?*
> **C:** *You can make that happen!*
> **H:** *Carry on.*

IV. What would you need to be the best teacher you could be? More money? More time? More training? Smaller classes? More administrative support? What can you do to help make that happen?

V. If you could be sure your students learned one thing in their time with you, what would it be?

ACKNOWLEDGMENTS

Thanks to the lovely editors Trish Boczkowski and Karen Kosztolnyik, as well as everyone else at Gallery Books who helped with this project, including Jen Bergstrom, Jennifer Weidman, Becky Prager, Lisa Litwack, Ela Schwartz, and Martha Schwartz; Cait Hoyt and Jonathan Swaden at CAA; Daniel Greenberg at Levine Greenberg Rostan; Eric Weissler; and teachers everywhere!

NOTES

I. Truth Telling

1. Guy Trebay, "At the Met Gala, a Strict Dress Code," *New York Times*, April 23, 2014, http://www.nytimes.com/2014/04/24/fashion/at-the-met-gala-a-strict-dress-code.html?_r=0#.

2. Jennifer Finney Boylan, "Save Us From the SAT," *New York Times*, March 6, 2014, http://www.nytimes.com/2014/03/07/opinion/save-us-from-the-sat.html?_r=0.

3. Kaplan, "The 100 Most Common SAT Words," Washington Post Education Marketplace, http://www.washingtonpost.com/wp-adv/eduadv/kaplan/kart_ug_sat100.html.

4. Tamar Lewin, "Revised SAT Won't Include Obscure Vocabulary Words," *New York Times*, April 16, 2014, http://www.nytimes.com/2014/04/16/education/revised-sat-wont-include-obscure-vocabulary-words.html?smid=tw-nytimes&_r=0.

NOTES

II. Empathy

1. Rebecca Adams, "Tim Gunn on Transgender Models, His Sexuality & Finding Role Models," *Huffington Post*, February 24, 2014, http://www.huffingtonpost.com/2014/02/24/tim-gunn-transgender-models_n_4830882.html.

2. Kate McDonough, "Tim Gunn Says He Feels 'Conflicted' about Transgender Models," *Salon*, Februay 24, 2014, http://www.salon.com/2014/02/24/tim_gunn_says_he_feels_conflicted_about_transgender_models/.

3. Parker Marie Molloy, "Tim Gunn 'Conflicted' about Trans Models," Advocate.com, February 25, 2014, http://www.advocate.com/politics/transgender/2014/02/25/tim-gunn-conflicted-about-trans-models.

4. Our Lady J, *"RuPaul's Drag Race* and the Danger of Overpolicing Language," HuffPost Gay Voices, *Huffington Post*, April 14, 2014, http://www.huffingtonpost.com/our-lady-j/rupauls-drag-race_b_5148719.html.

5. "The Hounding of a Heretic," *The Dish*, April 3, 2014, http://dish.andrewsullivan.com/2014/04/03/the-hounding-of-brendan-eich/.

III. Asking

1. Joyce Tyldesley, *Cleopatra: Last Queen of Egypt* (New York: Perseus, 2008).